CAR REGISTI

in the British

by Peter Robson

A 1 (London, 1903). Earl Russell's Napier car.
This was the first London County Council mark but not the first
mark to be issued in the British Isles.

C 75 (West Riding of Yorkshire, 1904)
KT 2059 (Kent, 1914)

Veteran, Edwardian and Vintage

Early Days

Transport numbering was not a new idea when car registration was introduced in the British Isles in 1903. The railway companies had for many years issued their locomotives and other rolling stock with identification numbers and as early as the eighteen-seventies British fishing boats had displayed numbers made up of one, two or three letters followed by numerals (a system still in use today), the letters depicting the port of registration such as M for Milford Haven, GY for Grimsby, BRD for Broadford, etc.

The motor car, after many years of invention and experimentation, became generally available in Britain in the mid eighteen-nineties and, as more and more motorists took to the roads, crimes such as speeding or otherwise upsetting fellow road users occurred with ever-increasing frequency. However, vehicles at that time did not display numbers and their drivers usually wore helmets and goggles so it was often impossible for the police to identify and apprehend miscreants. The Motor Car Act of 1903 therefore required all drivers to be licensed and all vehicles to be registered and to carry number plates. Registration and licensing of cars and their drivers were to be the responsibility of the county, county borough and larger Scottish burgh councils.

It is impossible to be precise about the place and date of the world's first vehicle registrations. Numberplates were reputedly used in Paris in 1893 and 'personalised' plates with owners' initials were issued in Hungary in 1895. The following year the state of Baden in Germany introduced registrations consisting of the initial of the town of issue followed by a numeral.

In the United Kingdom, which then comprised Great Britain and all of Ireland, a scheme of registration marks was devised using a single letter or pair of letters to identify the council of registration followed by a number of up to three digits (1 - 999) but this plan was soon extended to four digits (1-9999). In England - also including Glasgow and Lanarkshire - the councils were listed in order of population size at the 1901 census, starting with single-letter A for London (population 4,536,541) down to Y for Somerset (population 385,111), then double-letters AA for Hampshire (population 364,445) down to FP for Rutland (population 19,709). Numberplates could be either oblong or square. The letters and numerals, $3^{1}/_{2}$ inches high and $2^{1}/_{2}$ inches wide (except for I and 1), were to be white on a black background. These dimensions were halved for motorcycle plates.

Single letter S and double letter combinations with G, S and V - for example AS, CV, EG - were not initially included in the main scheme and were reserved for Scotland. Letters I and Z were also excluded, being kept for use in Ireland, and Q was not issued at all until many years later. Other omissions were DD (probably thought unsuitable as it had religious connotations as Doctor of Divinity), DT (short for Delirium Tremens, an illness resulting from chronic alcoholism) and ER (reason unknown, but probably because it stood for Edwardus Rex = King Edward who was the reigning monarch at the time).

In Scotland a different system was devised. Edinburgh, as the capital, was given S (for Scotland), after which the counties were listed in alphabetical order using combinations containing the letter S, starting with SA for Aberdeeenshire and continuing (with a few exceptions) to SY for Midlothian, then AS for Nairn, BS for Orkney, and so on as far as PS for Zetland (Shetland). Thereafter the larger burghs (population over 50,000) were listed, also in alphabetical order, from Aberdeen Burgh Council (RS) to Partick Burgh Council (YS).

A similar scheme was adopted in Ireland using combinations containing the letter I, starting with IA for County Antrim down to IZ for County Mayo, then continuing from AI for County Meath to NI for County Wicklow, followed by county boroughs Belfast (OI) to Waterford (WI). Exceptions to the rule were IG, II, IQ, IS, IV, GI, QI, SI and VI which were not included in this initial allocation.

Most councils started issuing their numbers at 1 and progressed numerically, regardless of the type of vehicle. Others, until 1920, issued one set of numbers for cars and another (or two others) for motorcycles and/or heavy motor cars (lorries, buses, etc) so that in some areas, such as Cardiganshire, a car and a motorcycle would both carry identical registrations. A few authorities, like Norfolk, ran a separate series of numbers beginning with zero (e.g. AH 0673) for heavy motor cars.

AH 0743 (Norfolk, c.1920). A few authorities issued a separate series with extra zero for heavy vehicles.

Some early owners

Although the law did not require motor vehicles to be registered until 1 January 1904, many authorities began issuing registration marks in the autumn of 1903. It is impossible now to say which was the very first mark to be issued because many of the original council records have been destroyed. Some of the earliest were Hastings (DY 1), Buckinghamshire (BH 1) and Somerset (Y 1) issued on 23, 24 and 25 November 1903 respectively. The most famous, but by no means the first, was A 1, issued by London County Council. Earl Russell (elder brother of the philosopher Bertrand Russell), who was a keen motorist, sat up all night in order to be first in the queue when allocation of the A series was begun in December 1903. He secured A 1 for his Napier car but later regretted owning the number as the police could easily identify him when guilty of speeding.

Reservations for small or distinctive numbers were made by many other people, the lowest often being allocated to local members of the aristocracy or those who held important posts in the community. FX 1, for example, was issued to the Lord-Lieutenant of Dorset, EY 1 to the Chairman of Anglesey County Council, ST 9 to the Vice-Lieutenant of

Inverness-shire. Many early numbers have been passed down from generation to generation and some (including the above) are still retained in the same families today.

Undesirable Registrations

The compilers of the first list of allocations had overlooked the undesirability of the combinations BF and DF. Some motorists in Dorset, not wishing to appear 'bloody fools', objected to the letters BF so the county council applied for a different combination. In December 1904 they were granted FX, the next available code, instead and any motorists who wished to change were allowed to do so. In practice about half of the original BF owners preferred to keep their numbers. The series terminated at BF 162 and disappeared altogether as a result of the 1920 Roads Act when all remaining BF numbers were replaced.

A similar situation occurred in Northampton. The borough council was originally allotted DF (short, in those days, for 'damned fool') and likewise applied to have the mark changed. In their case, however, instead of being given the next available combination they were granted NH, quite out of sequence. This was the first example of a two-letter mark being deliberately issued to correspond with the name of the council, i.e. NortHampton, although the same thing had already happened by coincidence (BH to Buckinghamshire, BN to Bolton, CE to Cambridgeshire and DR to Devonport).

Running out of Numbers

By May 1905 the largest council, London, had reached the end of its original series (A) and was allotted a new mark LC relevant to its name (London County), i.e. the next number after A 9999 was LC 1. The LC series was followed in November 1906 by LN (LondoN) and subsequently by other combinations beginning with the letter L.

It was now realised that some of the larger councils would need several different marks to accommodate the high quantity of vehicles being registered. A scheme of 'block' allocations was adopted to give such councils plenty of scope for the future. Thus London eventually issued almost all the two-letter marks beginning with L (the exceptions being LJ and the Scottish/Irish combinations LG, LI, LS, LV and LZ).

6

Early Dorset cars. FX was allocated after complaints about BF.
The owner on the right (BF 117) has chosen to keep the old-style number.

The next authority to run out of numbers (in 1912) was Middlesex. Again, a place-related mark MX was allotted, followed by MC and thirteen other M's. The next year, four more councils required new marks and were given blocks: Birmingham followed the O series with OA and fourteen more O's, Kent acquired ten K's beginning with KT, Manchester followed N with NA to NF inclusive and Surrey followed P with PA to PL.

Among other councils with blocks of similar marks were West Riding of Yorkshire (WR, WY, WT, WU, WW, WX), Glasgow (G, GA, GB, GD, GE, GG), Sheffield (W, WA, WB, WE, WJ), Lancashire (TB, TC, TD, TE, TF, TJ) and Somerset (Y, YA, YB, YC, YD).

By 1920, London had exhausted all its L marks and was then allotted almost the complete series beginning with X. When these had been used, blocks beginning with Y, U and G were allocated. London's last combination JJ, issued in 1932, was its seventy fifth mark.

New Boroughs

After the initial allocations in 1903 (A to FP) several towns which had hitherto not been registration authorities became county boroughs and needed new marks. The first of these, in October 1904, were Blackpool and Tynemouth (FR and FT) and between 1905 and 1915 twelve more county boroughs were created in England and Wales. In the alphabetical sequence of marks, FU and FW were missed out, FX was allocated to Dorset to replace BF (see above) and combinations beginning with G had been reserved for Scotland. The new boroughs were given the marks FY, HA-HF, HH, HJ, HL-HN. Until 1964 (see page 21) the only other county borough to be created was Doncaster in 1927. It received the 'name-related' mark DT which had previously been omitted. In Scotland the towns of Motherwell and Wishaw were combined in 1920 to form a large burgh which was allocated GM (Scottish G plus, presumably, M for Motherwell).

From 1915 onwards, starting with HK, allocation of marks to smaller authorities needing new series was basically in alphabetical order but there were very many exceptions, apart from the councils with 'blocks'. All the non-Scottish and non-Irish marks beginning with J were missed out in the normal sequence. The K's belonged to Liverpool and Kent, and most of the L's to London. By 1921 the N's had been reached, and the P's by 1922.

New marks for English authorities were eventually in such short supply that in 1927 the spare combinations of G and V, previously reserved for Scotland, were issued south of the border. VG, for example, was allotted to Norwich, LG to Cheshire, TV to Nottingham. Finally the J series was broached in 1928.

Ireland

Although what is now the Republic of Ireland ceased to be part of the United Kingdom in 1921 the original numbering scheme continued to be used there until 1986 (see page 25).

The first Irish authority to complete its initial allocation was Belfast in 1921 which followed its existing OI with the next available mark in the Irish series XI. Dublin County Borough, originally allocated RI, followed later the same year with YI and in 1927 with ZI. Thereafter, AZ, BZ, etc. to YZ were issued by authorities in Northern Ireland; Z and most of ZA to ZY by authorities in the Republic of Ireland. ZG, ZS and ZV (having 'Scottish' endings) were missed out initially, as GI, IS, IV and SI had been, but these were all used later. The single letter I and combinations IG, II and VI were never issued.

CHAPTER
TWO

Three Letters and Reversals

1932 Onwards

By 1932, all the two-letter combinations in Great Britain (England, Wales and Scotland) except OO, WC and those containing letter Q, had been allocated so a new three-letter scheme was adopted to provide further registration marks for those councils which had used all their available numbers. In the case of some of the smaller Scottish authorities - Bute (SJ), Clackmannanshire (SL), Kinross (SV), Nairn (AS), Orkney (BS), Peebles (DS), Selkirkshire (LS), Shetland (PS) and Sutherland (NS) - this situation did not arise as so few registrations were issued that they were still using just their two-letter codes until the 1960s.

In Great Britain, when a council reached the end of its two-letter series it continued with three letters consisting of a prefix letter followed by the original mark. For example, when Hastings council reached DY 9999 in 1937 it began at ADY 1. Each of the three-letter series ran from 1 to 999 so that in the above example ADY 999 was followed by BDY 1 and so on. As I, Q and Z were not used as prefix letters, this scheme normally provided a further 22,977 numbers for each two-letter series.

Authorities with several two-letter marks usually issued all of these with an A prefix, followed by all with a B prefix, etc. Most councils, like Cardiff (BO, UH, KG), progressed in alphabetical order of original marks (ABO, AKG, AUH, BBO, BKG, BUH, CBO, etc.) but some, like Southampton (CR, TR, OW), adopted the same order in which their two-letter marks had been used (ACR, ATR, AOW, BCR, BTR, BOW, CCR, etc.). There were many exceptions to the general rule, with certain series issued ahead of their time or missed out altogether.

The first authority to issue a three-letter combination was Staffordshire (ARF) in July 1932. This was followed by Middlesex (AMY) and Surrey (APA) in October of the same year and Cheshire (ALG) and Kent (AKE) in November.

RPH 848 (Surrey, 1952)   *AYC 518 (Somerset, 1935)*

Unlike two-letter combinations, those with three letters sometimes spelled a rude or otherwise unacceptable word and such combinations were generally omitted. These unissued series fell into several catagories such as toilet, bodily or sexual (ARS, AWC - a water closet, BOG, BUB, BUM, CNT, COC, COK, FUC, FUK, FUX, LAV, MAS - Gaelic for buttock, POE, POX, SEX, UWC), animal (APE, ASS, BUG, HOG), religious (GOD, JEW, DUW - Welsh for God) or just generally offensive (ABF - a bloody fool, BAS - Gaelic for death, BBF, DAM, KIL, MUK, NAZ, NBG - no bloody good, SOD, SOT and UBF).

Several other doubtful combinations, however, were not frowned on, such as MUC, PEE, POO and WOG although the last of these has now been added to the list of banned marks. Fashions change: what was once offensive is now thought acceptable and vice versa. Examples of many of the combinations originally unissued have recently been sold in the government 'Classic', 'Custom' and 'Select' series (see page 32).

Some other three-letter marks were omitted in the early days on the grounds of confusion rather than offence. AHO and BHO, which would normally have been issued by Hampshire council, were left out allegedly because they might have been misread for Norfolk or Buckinghamshire heavy vehicle numbers, e.g. AHO 375 might have been confused with AH 0375. Other omitted series were USN (confusion with United States Navy), XXX (confusion with police call sign) and DWO. The combination GPO which would normally have been allocated to West Sussex was instead used for General Post Office vehicles and issued by London County Council. MAN was specially reserved for the Isle of Man (see page 39).

Reversals (1953 onwards)

The system of two letters followed by up to four digits, then three letters followed by up to three digits, was adequate until 1953 but by then some councils were again running out of available numbers. It was decided to introduce a new format - of numerals followed by letters - for use when all other series had been exhausted. The rules were not rigidly laid down so some councils issued reverse single-letter marks, some double-letter, some triple-letter and some combinations of these.

As with the original three-letter series, Staffordshire issued the first of the reversed numbers, with 1000 E (and not 1 E as might be expected, because of possible confusion with trade plates, see pages 40 and 41) appearing in April 1953 followed by 1 ARE three months later. Meanwhile Middlesex had started reverse H (also at 1000) in June. The first reversed double-letter mark was 1 WB issued by Sheffield in May 1957. The reverse system worked satisfactorily if somewhat haphazardly until 1960 by which time Staffordshire was again running out of numbers - a problem solved by resuscitating the old 'banned' BF series (starting at CBF). Similarly, in 1961 Essex County Council had almost exhausted its stock of numbers. There were still two double-letter marks which

OO 6006 (Essex, 1961)   *8996 EL (Bournemouth, 1960)*
Now cherished

had never been issued - OO and WC - so these were allocated to Essex which issued first OO 1 to OO 9999, then AOO to YOO with letters first, followed by BWC to YWC (WC, AWC and UWC were omitted). The three-letter sequences were then reversed, starting with 1 AOO.

Ireland

Irish authorities also adopted three-letter and reverse formats when their original two-letter marks became exhausted, but the sequences of issue were different from those in Great Britain.

In Northern Ireland the original series of two-letter marks were reversed, starting with numerals and ending with letters. For example the sequence in Armagh was IB 1 to IB 9999, LZ 1 to LZ 9999, XZ 1 to XZ 9999, then reversed IB, reversed LZ and reversed XZ. Three-letter marks were then issued using one two-letter series all the way through. Thus, in the above example, after 9999 XZ, the first three-letter mark (AIB) was introduced but, unlike Great Britain, each three-letter series carried on to 9999. When AIB was completed, BIB was begun - and not ALZ as might be expected. This was only begun when YIB came to an end. It is perhaps worth noting that only Irish authorities (in both Northern Ireland and the Republic) used I as a prefix, e.g. in Omagh HJI was followed by IJI followed by JJI (see also pages 18 and 19).

The pattern was again different in the Republic. There the original two-letter series was followed by the three-letter format with numerals up to 999. For example, County Meath issued AI 1 to AI 9999, followed by ZN 1 to ZN 9999, then AAI 1 to AAI 999, BAI 1 to BAI 999, etc. As well as I, the letter Z was used as a prefix (unlike the rest of the British Isles), so that in the above example YAI 999 was followed by ZAI 1 to ZAI 999, then AZN , followed by BZN, etc. When all the three-letter marks were exhausted the two-letter marks were reversed, e.g. 1 AI onwards. Those authorities which used all their reversed two-letter marks followed these with reversed three-letters, e.g. County Kerry followed 9999 ZX with 1 AIN.

As in Great Britain, some authorities in Ireland started their reversed series at a higher number than 1 to prevent confusion with trade plates.

 (continued on page 21)

R 6244 (Derbyshire, 1921)

BE 964 (Lincolnshire (Lindsey), c.1908)

UN 945 (Denbighshire, 1927)

IK 52 (Co. Dublin, 1903/4)

SS 2921 (East Lothian, 1929)

CTY 761 (Northumberland, 1948)

GLI 606 (Co Westmeath, 1966)

339 EWN (Swansea, 1963)

1735 ME (Middlesex, 1960)

4348 F (Essex, 1957)

284-KIM (Co Galway, 1981)

NFR 147G (Blackpool, 1968)   **CSP 596V** (Dundee, 1979)

FFA 1L (Burton-on-Trent, 1973)   **MGW 484L** (London, 1972)
Now cherished

Registration marks of vehicles manufactured from 1 January 1973 onwards must be displayed on reflective plates (white front, yellow rear). Black plates with white/silver characters may be used on vehicles manufactured before that date if preferred.

MGB 1Y (Glasgow, 1982)   **N112 VBL** (Reading, 1995)
with 2001-style characters.

SCY 1J
(Cornwall, 1971)
Y39 SCY
(Truro, 2001)
SCY was originally issued by Swansea Borough Council in 1958 (without year letter) and in 1969 (with year suffix G).

When vehicle taxation was introduced in the Isles of Scilly (off the south-west coast of Cornwall) in 1971, the SCY combination (from J suffix onwards) was specially reserved for use there.

SCY 1J was the first Scilly Isles number, and Y39 SCY was the last.

P816 BUG (Leeds, 1996-7). BUG, which was formerly a 'banned' combination, has also appeared in recent years in DVLA Classic and Custom auctions (2 BUG, BUG 3, BUG 10W, etc). It is popular with owners of VW 'new' Beetles, e.g. L333 BUG (DVLA Select).

SL02 VJX (Edinburgh, 2002)   **LF52 ABV** (Wimbledon, 2002)

CK51 WZD (Cardiff, 2002)
Letter Z first appeared in Great Britain's
marks in September 2001.

HW51 JYF (Portsmouth, 2001)
HW marks are reserved for use in the
Isle of Wight

PO02 NRX (Preston, 2002)

JU52 KJK (DVLA Select, 2002) New-format marks beginning J, T and U have
not been allocated to any specific Local Office. Many of them are offered for sale
by DVLA as Select marks.

OIL 2336
(Enniskillen, 1997)
Cherished

Popular with cherished number enthusiasts throughout the United Kingdom, Enniskillen (Co Fermanagh) marks ending in IL give attractive combinations such as BIL, GIL, HIL, JIL, OIL, WIL, etc.

Northern Ireland marks have no year-identifiers and are favoured by many vehicle owners in Great Britain who wish to disguise the age of their cars. Several Northern Ireland combinations are also attractive because they spell words or initials such as BAZ, GAZ, JAZ, MBZ (a favourite with Mercedes Benz owners), LUI, NIB, RIB, etc.

All Northern Ireland marks contain the letter I or the letter Z (or both).

AJZ 3945 (Downpatrick, 2002)   **IUI 9752** (Londonderry,1998)

MJI 2465 (Omagh, 1989)

JIW 570 (Coleraine, 1988)
Cherished

JIB 1608 (Armagh, 1986)
Cherished

HKZ 2898 (Ballymena, 2001)

ICZ 6696 (Belfast, 2001)

Of the eight Local Vehicle Licensing
Offices in Northern Ireland,
Enniskillen will be the first to use
up all its available 'forward' numbers.
When the end of the YIL series is
reached (i.e. YIL 9999) it is likely
that reversed three-letter marks will be
started at 1 AIL (then to 9999 AIL,
1 BIL, etc.).

Numberplates used on vehicles registered in the United Kingdom can include, at the left hand end, an extra panel or strip depicting the symbol of the European Union - a circle of twelve stars on a blue background - with the letters GB below the symbol. This is recognised internationally as denoting UK origin and can be used instead of an oval GB plate or sticker (see page 102) when travelling abroad.

Alternatively one of four other national identifiers can legally be displayed on the left hand end of the numberplate with appropriate letters beneath. These are the cross of St George with ENG (for England), the red dragon with CYM (for Wales), the saltire with SCO (for Scotland) and the Union flag with letters GB (for the UK).

However, as these are not official international identifiers, a separate GB oval plate or sticker should also be displayed when the vehicle is used outside the UK.

So long as the flags/emblems follow the above descriptions the exact designs can be varied. The kind illustrated above right can be obtained from Regtransfers (www.regtransfers.co.uk) (postal address on page 107).

Current numberplates in the Republic of Ireland include the European Union symbol and international letters IRL (see pages 48-9). Those in the Isle of Man include the three-legged Manx emblem and international letters GBM on a red background (see pages 52-3).

 CHAPTER
THREE

Suffixes and Prefixes

Year Letters

By the early nineteen-sixties it was clear that the existing system in Great Britain would not last much longer so a new one was devised which would be capable of providing registration marks, if used in both forward and reversed formats, for at least another forty years.

Marks issued under the new scheme would consist of three letters (the last two of which, as before, denoted the issuing authority), then a number from 1 to 999 and then a suffix letter denoting the year of issue. As some councils, by 1963, were in urgent need of a new supply of marks, the first suffix letter (A) was allocated for that year, followed by B for 1964 and so on. As the maximum number of characters on a number plate was now increased from six to seven (e.g. CKG 297B) the dimensions of the letters and numerals were reduced to a width of $2^{1}/_{4}$ inches and a height of $3^{1}/_{8}$ inches.

In practice, only fourteen authorities used the A suffix (but see pages 33 and 34), the first being Middlesex with the series beginning AHX 1A issued in February 1963. The majority of councils started with the B suffix in 1964 (e.g. Eastbourne AHC 1B, Surrey APA 1B) but some delayed issuing year letters until January 1965 (e.g. Inverness AST 1C, South Shields ACU 1C).

After the introduction of year letters, two new Scottish burghs and three new English county boroughs were created and were allotted former London marks from XA to XF. Thus Kirkcaldy issued from AXA 1A in 1963; Coatbridge from AXB 1B, Solihull from AXC 1B and Luton from AXD 1B and AXE 1B in 1964; and Torbay from AXF 1F in 1968.

The letters I, O, Q and Z were never intended to be used as suffixes and it was also decided to omit U in view of the possible confusion with V. This meant that the new system would last until the end of 1983 if kept going the same way. However, it was decided in 1967, for the benefit of the motor trade, that each year letter period should begin on 1 August instead of 1 January. Suffix F was started in August 1967, G in August 1968 and so on until the Y suffix numbers were completed in July 1983.

Meanwhile new reflective numberplates had been introduced in the U.K. in 1967 and were made compulsory for all vehicles manufactured on or after 1 January 1973. These plates were white (front) or yellow (rear) with black letters and numerals. Reflective plates, white front and red rear, had also been introduced in the Republic of Ireland in 1969 on an optional basis.

Centralisation (1974-1978)

The planning of a major change in the organisation of motor vehicle licensing and registration began in 1965 and was implemented in the Vehicle and Driving Licences Act of 1969. A computerised Driver and Vehicle Licensing Centre (DVLC) was opened in Swansea in 1974, supported by eighty-one new regional Local Vehicle Licensing Offices (LVLOs, later - in Great Britain - renamed Vehicle Registration Offices and now called DVLA Local Offices). During the years 1974 to 1978 all records for currently licensed vehicles were transferred from the offices of county, county borough and Scottish burgh councils (known as Local Taxation Offices) to Swansea for entry on the central computer, the old-style log books being sent to Swansea to be replaced by computer-generated V5 registration documents. The last council licensing offices closed on 31 March 1978.

The new Local Vehicle Licensing Offices generally took over the registration marks of the nearest old authorities. For example, Preston LVLO issued marks formerly allocated to local councils in the surrounding area (BV from Blackburn, CK and RN from Preston, CW and HG from Burnley, and FR and FV from Blackpool). This procedure was not universal: several marks were transferred to LVLOs in busy areas from quite unrelated councils (e.g. GS transferred from Perth to Luton, JM from Westmorland to Reading).

Meanwhile decisions had to be made regarding the future of the large stocks of registers and other documents, many dating back to 1903, which were still stored at local council offices. The fate of these items varied greatly from place to place. In some areas they were completely or partially destroyed (including London C.C. whose records have all disappeared except for one solitary register from 1917) whilst in others they were carefully preserved and placed in local archives, such as those for Radnorshire kept at the Powys Record Office in Llandrindod Wells.

Ireland

Northern Ireland followed a similar pattern of centralisation with the opening of the DVLNI Vehicle Licensing Central Office in Coleraine in 1973, supported by eight Local Vehicle Licensing Offices. Year letters were not favoured and the issue of registration marks has followed a relatively simple pattern which is still in operation (three letters followed by up to four digits). In the Republic the existing system without year letters continued until the end of 1986. From 1 January 1987 a completely different format was introduced for new vehicles (see pages 25 and 94).

Year Letters Reversed (1983-2001)

In 1983 it was time for another change in registration marks in Great Britain and, as in 1953, the existing pattern was reversed. From 1 August 1983 the year letter (prefix) came first, followed by up to three numerals, then three letters. The A prefix ran from August 1983 to July 1984 (e.g. A134 FDC issued by Middlesbrough licensing office), then B from August 1984 to July 1985 (e.g. B280 KPF issued by Guildford), etc. This sequence lasted until prefix S which began on 1 August 1998. Thereafter the letter changes were made in March and September, so T began in March 1999, V in September 1999, W in March 2000, X in September 2000 and Y in March 2001.

In anticipation of the possible future sale of attractive registrations, numbers 1 to 20 (and sometimes other numbers) in each prefix series were withheld, so that those issued in the normal way started at 21 (e.g.A21 JEC, B21 KPF, L21 AKH).

In 1994 a new system called Automated First Registration and Licensing (AFRL) was introduced in Great Britain whereby registration of new vehicles could be carried out by dealers linked by computer through the manufacturers to DVLA. This means that many first registrations are not now dealt with by DVLA Local Offices.

CHAPTER FOUR

New Systems

New-style numbers in Great Britain

Between 1980 and 1997, forty-one of the original Local Vehicle Licensing Offices in Great Britain (i.e. England, Scotland and Wales) were closed, their business being transferred to neighbouring offices, and from January 2001 the remaining forty were officially renamed DVLA Local Offices.

As the last prefix (Y) was due to run out by the end of August 2001 a completely new format was devised which would provide registration marks for a further forty-nine or, if 'reversed', ninety-nine years.

The country was divided into nineteen areas, each of which was given a local memory tag, e.g. A for Anglia, S for Scotland, as the first letter of the registration mark. The DVLA Local Offices in each area were then given two-letter identifiers beginning with the local memory tag. Thus London's three offices were allotted LA to LJ (Wimbledon), LK to LT (Stanmore) and LU to LY (Sidcup). The letters I, Q and Z were not to be used in this two-letter system and the combinations FO, FU, MN and NF were also omitted.

Instead of year letters, a system of numbering has been adopted for use until February 2050 to identify the date of issue of a registration mark. From March to August each year the last two digits of the year are used, e.g. from March to August 2002 the age identifier is 02. For the succeeding months September to February, 50 is added on, e.g. from September 2002 to February 2003 the age identifier is 52 (i.e. 02 + 50). This system, if continued in the same way, will operate until the period September 2049 to February 2050 (age identifier 99). The first of these age identifiers (51) was issued between September 2001 and February 2002 (see table on page 76).

Each registration mark in the new system consists of seven characters: two letters (local office identifier), two digits (age identifier) and three letters (excluding I and Q but including, for the first time in Great Britain, the letter Z). For example, BV02 DDL signifies a mark issued by Birmingham local office between March and August 2002.

Numberplates in the new format will continue to be reflective white (front) and reflective yellow (rear) but stricter rules now apply about the kind of lettering used. An official font (typeface) based on the 'Charles Wright Font' has been adopted, to which all new-style numberplates must conform.

```
0123456789
ABCDEFGHJKLMN
OPQRSTUVWXYZ
```

New official font

Ireland

This new scheme was not adopted in Northern Ireland which is continuing the system already in operation, i.e. three letters followed by up to four digits.

In the Republic of Ireland the old UK series of marks has been replaced by an entirely new system. All new vehicles from January 1987 onwards have been issued with marks made up of two digits (the last two digits of the year of registration) followed by one or two letters (signifying the county or city of registration) followed by up to six digits. Thus 91-KE-515 signifies a vehicle registered in County Kildare in 1991. Both front and rear plates are reflective white. Some vehicles first registered before 1987 are re-registered with new-style marks, e.g. 73-D-2. For more details see page 94.

 CHAPTER

FIVE

Cherished Numbers

1903-1920

The enthusiasm for owning interesting or unusual car registrations is as old as registration itself. From the very start many people were keen to have the lowest possible numbers, and many more subsequently have wished to keep these numbers in the family by transferring them from one car (now known as the donor vehicle) to another (known as the recipient or receiving vehicle). The term 'cherished numbers' was first used in the nineteen-twenties and is now the accepted name for registrations which have a personal significance. There have been many other reasons for owning a distinctive number: some motorists favour their own initials or the initials of their company; some like numbers relevant to the county or town where they live; some derive amusement from combinations of letters and numbers which 'spell' a word. There are also some who regard their registrations as investments.

The transfer of registration marks from vehicle to vehicle, though not always directly, happened soon after the first cars had been registered in 1903. Just as at present, when a vehicle was scrapped or exported, its registration mark was made void, i.e. cancelled. In the early days of motoring, however, the void number was kept on the authority's files and often re-issued to another vehicle later on.

When a vehicle was sold, its mark could either be kept with the vehicle (as it normally is nowadays) or made void, in which case the mark could then be reissued to a different owner for a different vehicle. An example of this latter course of action was AJ 24, issued by North Riding of Yorkshire council in 1903 for a Lanchester car belonging to Frank Green. He sold the car in February 1910 and the number was cancelled. Four weeks later the same number was reissued to Oswald Smith for a Triumph motorcycle.

This procedure did not suit a great many motorists, particularly those who owned a low or interesting number and who wished to retain the original when changing cars. As transfers directly from vehicle to vehicle were not permitted by some councils, owners were able to overcome the problem by having the number of their old car cancelled in the normal way, then reapplying to the authority for the same number again, as a completely new transaction, when registering their new car. While this procedure was strictly adhered to by some authorities, others were prepared to transfer the numbers directly for a fee of one shilling (5p).

1920-1955

The reissuing of cancelled (void) numbers was stopped as a result of the Roads Act of 1920. The gist of the regulation was that a vehicle had to retain its original number (or, if already registered at the end of 1920, the number it was currently carrying) until it was either scrapped or exported. This meant that owners would no longer be able to transfer their numbers from car to car. The howls of protest from motorists soon resulted in an extra-statutory concession which allowed an owner who wished to transfer a registration from one vehicle to another to do so by application to the council (registration authority) and payment of a fee of £5.

Officially, until the rules were again changed in 1955, no void numbers were permitted to be reissued but the regulation was not always strictly adhered to. For example, when an appropriate registration was required for a new mayoral car in Northampton in the nineteen-thirties, NH 1, which had been cancelled and was not currently in use, was revived.

Place-related Marks

It is perhaps worth mentioning in passing that the two-letter codes still being allocated to authorities were sometimes deliberately chosen to match the place name. Some of these are noted in Chapter 1 (pages 6, 7 and 8) and during the twenties and early thirties several more appeared, including DV (Devon), KH (Kingston-upon-Hull), LV (Liverpool), RD (Reading), NL (Northumberland), TY also for Northumberland (Tyneside) and VT for Stoke-on-Trent - the federation of the 'Five Towns' of Burslem, Hanley, Longton, Stoke-upon-Trent and Tunstall.

To this list may be added MN and MAN used in the Isle of Man and SCY, specially reserved for the Isles of Scilly when motor taxation was introduced there in 1971.

1955-1962

After the Second World War there was a growing interest in cherished registrations, perhaps due partly to the increased media publicity given to famous personalities and their car numbers. Also various small books dealing with vehicle registrations were published, including 'Where's That Car From?' which listed all the then available letter combinations with their place of origin, and 'I-Spy Cars', a children's book which included several examples of famous people's registrations, such as Lord Brabazon's FLY 1.

Such was the demand for personalised numbers that, in 1955, the Ministry of Transport decided to allow local authorities to issue void numbers on request for a fee of £5. Hundreds of motorists took advantage of this concession and applied for numbers previously connected with their family or town or county, or numbers which included the initial letters of their names or had some other personal significance. Most of these numbers were short and of historical interest as the following examples show: AT 6, CG 29, CY 4, EJ 19, HW 23, M 6, PM 60, RO 1, SC 222, SW 1, T 8, TA 15, VM 13, WS 1, Y 8.

The concession was short-lived, however, for in 1962 the Ministry put a stop to the purchasing of old numbers from councils, claiming that the demand for cherished registrations had become so great that the authorities had neither time nor resources to deal with all the applicants. Transfers were still allowed but no more 'revived' numbers were issued.

Noël Woodall and Car Numbers Galaxy

It was at about this time that Noël Woodall, one of the most remarkable figures in the car registration world, appeared on the numbers scene. One day in 1960 he was driving into his home town of Blackpool and noticed that the car he was following bore the number BB 4. This set him wondering who owned the car and whether the number had any special significance to its owner.

Cherished marks: SAM 647 (originally Wiltshire, 1958)
and 5 PL (originally Surrey, 1962)

Noël visited the local reference library to enquire about books on car registrations but was told that no such book existed. So he decided to investigate the subject himself and sent out circulars to every garage in the AA book and every famous personality he could think of - about two thousand addresses altogether. The result was encouraging and provided him with enough material to compile 'Celebrities', his first book which was published by his own company Car Numbers Galaxy in 1962. This book was followed by 'Veterans' in 1963 and 'More Celebrities' in 1964. Since then he has produced more than twenty books on the subject of registrations, notably 'Car Numbers', a large and comprehensive directory of numbers and their owners. His late wife, Dawn, created the word 'autonumerology' - the study of car numbers.

Number Dealers

From 1962 onwards the cherished numbers scene changed radically. Although it was now no longer possible to purchase attractive registration marks directly from licensing authorities, the interest in personalised registrations continued to increase. The demand for 'old' numbers became even greater when year-letter suffixes were introduced in 1963/5, many motorists objecting to the their cars' ages being displayed.

The search was on for vehicles from which desirable marks could be transferred. Cherished registrations were becoming items of value, as was shown when RR 1 was sold in 1968 for £4,800. It was not long before several enterprising people had set themselves up as number dealers, buying registration marks belonging to old vehicles, advertising the numbers and selling them to interested clients. To avoid actually purchasing the old vehicles, many dealers kept the numbers they had bought on a stock of mopeds which were easy to store and could be used over and over again as temporary 'recipient' and 'donor' vehicles . In 1971, a group of these pioneer dealers formed the Personalised Numbers Dealers Association (PNDA) - now called the Cherished Numbers Dealers Association (CNDA) - to set high standards of trading among its members.

At that time, registration of vehicles was still the responsibilty of the county, county borough and larger burgh councils (local taxation offices) who continued to arrange transfers of numbers for a fee of £5. It was also possible (as it is at present) to keep a number on a retention certificate without putting it on a vehicle. The rules of transfer were then generally quite slack and it was possible in many cases for an applicant to visit the local licensing office carrying the registration document ('log book') of an old vehicle and ask for the number to be transferred to another vehicle. Often no check was made to establish whether the old vehicle actually existed, even though an inspection was meant to be carried out. Many attractive numbers were transferred in this way and saved from extinction.

When the centralisation of licensing began in 1974 and registration details were being sent from local councils to be entered on the computer at the Driver and Vehicle Licensing Centre (DVLC) in Swansea, it became possible to abuse the system by applying for allegedly missing log books or by feeding in altered log books. Again, in many instances the vehicles shown on the log books did not exist but the Swansea computer issued new and completely legitimate V5 registration documents which could then be used for subsequent transfers. The staff at Swansea eventually tumbled to these irregularities and decided to take action.

Industrial Action

On 29 July 1976 the Civil and Public Services Association and the Society of Civil and Public Servants (the licensing staff trade unions at Swansea) recommended its members, on the grounds of abuse of the system, to put an end to cherished transfers as from 4.00 p.m. the following day. The notice was strongly worded: 'It is intended that the ban on cherished transfers should be permanent, thus securing the complete abolition of the concession. To this end neither CPSA nor SCPS has plans for any compromise'. There was an immediate outcry, especially from the leading dealers who set up the Cherished Numbers Campaign Office in London to fight for the right to transfer numbers. One dealer, Tony Hill, organised his own demonstrations, including chaining himself to a lamp-post outside the DVLC in Swansea, amid impressive media attention.

After receiving votes at the DVLC on 10 November from the eighty-one licensing offices as to whether cherished transfers should be started again or banned altogether, a decision was finally reached. The following week the DVLC issued a press release to the effect that transfers were to be started again on 29 November.This was good news for dealers and motorists alike but it was tempered by a new set of stringent rules. The transfer fee was raised from £5 to £50 and no number could be transferred unless it had been registered to the same person for a minimum period of nine months. Furthermore, all retention certificates had to be surrendered by the end of January 1977, which meant that any retained numbers had to be put on vehicles before that date or be permanently lost. It was also decided that transfers from mopeds and motorcycles to cars would no longer be permitted. This last rule was waived in March 1978, and the nine month waiting period reduced to three months, following yet another campaign by Tony Hill. Cherished marks could still not be transferred from cars to motorcycles but this restriction was lifted in October 2001.

Meanwhile, the gradual changeover of records from local taxation offices to the DVLC computer continued and by the end of November 1983 the replacement of old log books by new V5 registration documents was complete. Any vehicles, except those of provable historic rarity, not registered on the computer after that date lost their orginal registration marks. This rule was later amended (see page 61).

Classic, Custom and Select

The government was by now well aware that a healthy profit could be made from cherished marks and in November 1989 the Secretary of State for Transport gave permission to the licensing centre at Swansea, now known as the Driver and Vehicle Licensing Agency (DVLA), to sell direct to the public. A selection of potentially valuable marks was made from previously unissued series ('The Classic Collection') and these were auctioned at Christie's in London on 14 December. The star of the show was 1 A which sold for a record price of £202,400, only to be beaten by K1 NGS which was to fetch £239,000 at an auction four years later.

The success of the 1989 sale resulted in more 'numberplate' auctions in various parts of the country and these are now held every few months, attracting those buyers who are able and willing to spend considerable amounts. Two other schemes have also been introduced by DVLA for the benefit of enthusiasts with more modest means. 'Custom' auctions (first held in June 2000) feature lower-price - and therefore not so attractive - numbers, often requested by members of the public, and 'Select' registrations (introduced in October 1990) are numbers which the customer can choose for him/herself and order via the telephone or internet. These numbers are either of the 'prefix' style consisting of a letter, a range of numerals specified by DVLA - usually low numbers or repeated ones like 444 - and three letters chosen by the customer, e.g. A12 JLP, or the 'new' style consisting of two letters, a year identifier and three letters, e.g. JR02 DAN. There are some combinations of letters which are banned because they might cause offence but very many of those previously omitted are now available including ABF, APE, AWC, BAS, BBF, BOG, BUB, BUG, CNT, HOG, LAV, MAS, MUK, NBG, POE, SOT and UBF (see page 10).

Collections

Some companies, and occasionally private individuals, have accumulated considerable collections of cherished marks over the years, for example J.C. Bamford Excavators Ltd with JCB marks on nearly one hundred of their vehicles, including JCB 1, and J.G.Fenn Ltd (business supplies company) of Stoke-on-Trent with JGF 28 and nine other JGF marks.

Cherished registrations are becoming increasingly popular, with about one-tenth of all newly-issued marks being specially chosen by their owners. For information about obtaining a cherished mark, see Chapter Nine (page 57).

 CHAPTER **LSL 855**
SIX

Replacements and Age-Related Marks

1903-1963

When a cherished registration mark is transferred from one vehicle to another, the first vehicle (the donor vehicle) is left without a mark. The issuing office then has to provide a replacement. Also, if a vehicle is permanently imported or has not been previously registered, such as a farm vehicle which has never before been driven on a public road or a military vehicle converting to civilian use, a spare mark needs to be found for it. Before the introduction of year letters in 1963 most councils simply issued the next available mark in the series they were currently using.

1963-1976

After conversion to year letters, replacement marks (or re-registrations) were issued with the appropriate letter, e.g. KDN 535L from York licensing office to replace a mark on a 1972/3 vehicle. This policy still continues, each authority keeping sets of spare marks from each year's (or half-year's) stock just for this purpose. For pre-1963 vehicles, replacements were usually created by continuing the old non-year-letter series. For example, Dudley council had reached 581 EFD in their normal numbering when they began using a year letter, starting with AFD 1B in July 1964. The old series from 582 EFD onwards was then used for replacements for older vehicles.

1976-1983

This policy, however, resulted in some of the replacement marks, which had low numbers and were attractive, being 'cherished' themselves. Following the strike of staff at DVLC in 1976 (see page 30) no more 'yearless' replacements were normally allowed. Instead, pre-1963 vehicles were given replacements with an A, B or C suffix. An exception was made in the case of veteran, Edwardian and vintage vehicles (pre 1931) which were given reissued EL and spare SL numbers, e.g. SL 9881 issued to a 1904 car. For some vehicles produced between 1931 and 1955, marks were created from the previously unused series WFX (followed by numerals) and DEL (preceded by numerals).

MSV 850 (Replacement mark. DVLC, 1985).

1983-1991

From 1983 the replacement rules were changed. Vehicles first registered between 1956 and 1963 were given marks with a A suffix, e.g. ADC 215A issued for a 1960 van. Pre-1905 (veteran) vehicles received unused numbers from the BS series, e.g. BS 8111 issued for a 1904 car. Vehicles manufactured between 1905 and 1930 (Edwardian and vintage) were given spare numbers from the DS series (also issued initially for veterans), e.g. DS 9940 issued for a 1929 car, and, from August 1992 onwards, the SV series, e.g. SV 5730 issued for a 1926 motorcycle. Vehicles dating from 1931 to 1955 received previously unused Scottish and Welsh marks beginning with the series ASV to YSV. Blocks of these marks, from 101 to 999, were allocated to each licensing office, e.g. GSV 101 to 300 (Dundee), VSV 501 to 700 (Reading), etc.

1991 onwards

The replacement policy was slightly revised again in 1991 when all post-1930 pre-1963 vehicles received replacements without year letters.

After ASV-YSV, these continued with CSU-YSU, BSK-YSK, GVS-YVS, TYJ-YYJ, KFF-YFF, GFO-TFO, VFO-YFO, PSY-YSY, ASJ-YSJ, ASL-YSL, AAS onwards, e.g. LSK 747 issued by Chelmsford office for a 1958 car. It was also decided that 'age-related' marks could not become 'cherished', and therefore a source of profit, so they were made non-transferrable, i.e. they could not be transferred from the vehicle for which they were issued (though some occasionally 'slip through the net').

Classic cars with recent age-related replacement marks are sometimes used in 'period' films set in pre-1963 days. The cars are usually quite authentic but their 'modern' numbers give them away!

Ireland

As Northern Ireland has not adopted year-identifiers its registration marks are 'ageless' so replacements are usually issued from the current series. The only exceptions are vehicles of true historic interest which are occasionally issued with unused marks from old series.

In the Republic of Ireland cherished transfers are not permitted. However, a vehicle over thirty years old needing to be newly registered (e.g. an old car imported from another country) can be issued with a mark in the series ZV followed by three or four (and, in the future, five) digits if the owner prefers this 'old-fashioned' style to the new format. Numberplates for ZV marks are black with white or silver characters.

421 HPY (Replacement mark. Middlesbrough, c.1976).

CHAPTER
SEVEN

Embassies, Islands and Others

Her Majesty the Queen

Her Majesty the Queen's official cars do not display registration plates.

Embassies

The official cars, based in London, of ambassadors of foreign countries (or high commissioners for Commonwealth countries) often carry specially allotted registration marks, usually incorporating the number 1, relating to the name of their country. These include 1 DAN (Denmark), 1 M (Malaysia), BEL 12E (Belize), SUD 1 (Sudan). An oval with the letters CD for 'Corps Diplomatique' is sometimes displayed on the car or the numberplate.

Cars of diplomatic and other staff of embassies and international organisations carry registrations consisting of three numbers denoting the embassy or high commission (101 onwards) or organisation (900 onward), followed by the letter D for diplomatic staff or X for accredited non-diplomatic staff, followed by three numbers, e.g. 135 D 309 (see also pages 100-1). When vehicles with this type of mark are sold they are re-registered with a mark in a normal series.

From 1984 onwards a small number of diplomatic cars were issued with RXS marks with year-prefix or -suffix appropriate to their age. These marks remained with their vehicles on disposal but are no longer used for diplomatic purposes.

Mayoral Cars

Many mayors, provosts and other county, city and town council dignitaries have 'cherished' or specially issued marks on their cars. A mayoral numberplate often includes the number 1 together with letters denoting the local issuing authority, such as U 1 (Leeds), 1 FD (Dudley), TS 1(Dundee), CDJ 1 (St Helens), or made up of suitable initials like RBK 1 (Royal Borough of Kingston upon Thames).

A few official council cars in Scotland carry marks which incorporate the single figure zero. These include G 0 and V 0 (Glasgow), HS 0 (East Renfrewshire), RG 0 (Aberdeen), S 0 (Edinburgh), SY 0 (Midlothian), and VS 0 (Inverclyde). The Lord Mayor of London has LM 0, particularly appropriate as LM is a London registration as well as standing for 'Lord Mayor'.

Letter Q

Marks incorporating the letter Q are issued in two quite distinct series. Since 1983, Q has been used in the same way as a year prefix, e.g. Q597 WVK, for vehicles whose date of manufacture is unknown, such as some imports, kit cars, or vehicles made up from parts of other vehicles. In Northern Ireland the QNI series is issued for the same purpose.

The other kind of Q mark is issued for temporarily imported vehicles which are either not required to be registered in their home countries, e.g. mopeds, or are displaying foreign numberplates which contain no western-style letters or numerals, e.g. those in Arabic script, etc. These marks were introduced in 1921 and comprised the series QA to QY followed by up to four digits. They were issued by London County Council and the AA and RAC motoring organisations, beginning with QQ which was followed by QA, QC, QS and then others in the Q series. The mark ZZ, now followed by five digits, is issued by the Automobile Association in the Republic of Ireland for the same purpose.

From the registration year 1981-1982, the Q marks in Great Britain were issued to coincide with the current year letter, e.g. QX followed by numerals for suffix X (1981-2), QY for suffix Y (1982-3). After this the series was issued in reverse form (e.g. 456 QD) with a second letter again coinciding with the year letter, e.g. numerals followed by QA for prefix A (1983-4), QB for prefix B (1984-5) to QY (March to August 2001). From September 2001 these marks continued in reverse form with the age-identifier number at the end, e.g. 123 Q02 issued between March and August 2002, etc .

XP Series

In 1993 a special series of marks was introduced for the temporary registration of vehicles involved in the Personal Export, New Means of Transport and Direct Export schemes and therefore exempt from VAT (Value Added Tax). These marks, intended to assist Customs and Excise in identifying the tax free status of the vehicles, were issued by eleven of the Vehicle Registration Offices and consisted of the year prefix followed by a three-digit number followed by three letters ending XP. The first of the three letters denoted the month of issue - AXP for January, BXP for February to HXP for August, then JXP for September to MXP for December, e.g. X268 KXP issued in October 2000.

When the new registration format was introduced in September 2001 (see page 24), marks beginning XA to XF replaced the XP series and are now issued by fifteen Local Offices. In this new system the letters XA signify the first month of each six-month period, XB the second month, etc. Thus XA51 (e.g. XA51 ABC) means a tax free export vehicle registered in September 2001, XB51 in October 2001, XC02 in May 2002, etc.

Channel Islands

Numberplates on the islands of Jersey, Guernsey and Alderney are similar to those in the U.K., with either white or silver British-style characters on a black background or black on reflective white (front) or yellow (rear) backgrounds.

Jersey registrations normally consist of the letter J followed by up to six digits but recently additional marks in the series JSY 1-999 have been available at auction. When cars are scrapped or withdrawn their registrations can be reissued.The official car of the Lieutenant-Governor of Jersey does not carry numberplates. Hire car numberplates include the letter H in silver or white on a red background

Guernsey registrations consist of up to five digits (but without a letter). Five-digit numbers from scrapped or withdrawn vehicles can be reissued and numbers with fewer digits can be obtained on payment of a fee (see page 62). The official car of the Lieutenant-Governor does not carry numberplates but his private cars are registered G 1 and G 2. The number 1 is used by the Bailiff. Hire cars carry a small yellow plate with black letter H in addition to their normal number. Alderney registrations consist of the letters AY followed by up to four digits.

Isle of Man

The two-letter British mark MN was reserved for the Isle of Man which started issuing registrations in 1906. In 1935, when this series had reached MN 9999, three-letter marks were issued in the mainland fashion except that MAN was used instead of AMN (MAN would normally have been issued by West Ham council in 1957). Thereafter the alphabetical sequence was followed from BMN 1 to YMN 999 but omitting SMN.

In 1959 reversed series were issued in the order 1 MN to 9999 MN, 1 MAN (in May 1964) to 999 MAN, then 1 BMN (in October 1964) to 999 YMN but again leaving out SMN. This was followed from 1971 to 1974 by a reissue of all available numbers from MN 1 to MN 9999.

The suffix-style numbering which had started in Great Britain in 1963 was then adopted, starting at MAN 2A (MAN 1A had already been specially issued) and continuing as far as MAN 999Y. The suffix letters, however, were simply used one after the other and did not signify the year of issue as on the mainland. Also, unlike the mainland, the letter U was used as a suffix but not the letter S. In 1979 the system was reversed, starting at A1 MAN, ending with Y999 MAN and including O1 MAN to O999 MAN and U1 MAN to U999 MAN but not prefix letter S.

Between May 1983 and August 1987 MAN 1000 to MAN 9999 and then 1000 MAN to 9999 MAN were issued, followed by the present system using BMN with suffixes (except O and S), then CMN with suffixes, etc.

Throughout all the Isle of Man number series the letters I, S and Z have been omitted. Numberplates have followed the normal UK style, first white or silver figures on a black background, then black on reflective white (front) and yellow (rear), until 1994 when new-style (optional) plates were introduced. These are of the reflective type but with hyphens and narrower characters, e.g. FMN-736-H, 7117-MAN. They include the Manx three-legged emblem and letters GBM on a red vertical strip at the left-hand end and the words 'Isle of Man' or 'Ellan Vannin' (Manx name for the island) in Celtic script above the number. Q plates, like those in Great Britain, are used for kit cars or vehicles of unknown age. e.g. Q-77-MAN.

The Lieutenant-Governor's cars are registered MAN 1 and MAN 2.

Trade Plates

Special registration marks, originally called General Identification Marks and now known as trade plates, are issued to motor manufacturers, agents and dealers to enable unlicensed vehicles to be driven lawfully on the roads. They are used temporarily for purposes such as test driving new cars or moving vehicles from one garage to another.

AE-B3 (Bristol, c.1904). General Identification Mark used by Bristol Carriage & Wagon Co. Ltd.

General Identification Marks (GIMs) were introduced in 1903, at the same time as ordinary registrations. Each issuing council was free to choose its own format for these, provided that the colouring was different from that used for normal plates, and that the council's index mark formed the first part of the number. The most popular format began with the index mark (e.g. BH for Buckinghamshire), followed by a letter or letters denoting the dealer or manufacturer, followed by a sequential number, each separate pair of plates used by the dealer or trader having their own number. Some authorities, including London, adopted a similar format but with the last two elements reversed. Others used the same letters for all their GIMs, frequently the initial letter of the authority (e.g. BB-N in

Newcastle upon Tyne) with sequential final numbers. A few authorities devised their own unique formats.

Although a red background with white characters was suggested for GIMs in a circular sent to councils in 1903 many authorities adopted other colouring schemes. Birmingham, for example, chose white characters on a blue background; London chose black characters on a white background.

General Identification Marks were standardised as a result of the Roads Act of 1920. All plates now had to be white with red characters and a red border, the numbers consisting of four figures between 0001 and 0999 together with the local index mark. The front numberplate included a holder for the licence card.

In 1923 the system was changed again and the terms 'trade licence' and 'trade plate' were now officially used. The new trade plates were issued in two different series - 'general' and 'limited', depending on the precise purpose for which they were allocated. General plates (high licence fee) were red with white characters; limited plates (much lower licence fee but with restrictions on how they could be used) were white with red characters. The marks usually consisted of a three digit number from 001 to 999 followed by a one-, two- or (very occasionally) three-letter code of the issuing council, e.g. 715 GC (London). In 1970 the practice of having two different types of plate was discontinued and all trade plates in the UK are now white with red characters.

The Isle of Man uses trade plates similar to those in the UK, i.e. red characters on a white background, with the letters MNA followed by three digits. Trade plates in Jersey are red with white characters (J followed by a short number). Guernsey and Alderney trade plates, with white characters on a black background, have short numbers preceded by T (general), Z (limited) or X (motorcycle).

A new type of trade plate was introduced in the Republic of Ireland in 1993. This is similar to the current format of normal Irish registrations (see page 94) but with characters in the reverse order, i.e. a number followed by the county or city code followed by the last two digits of the year of issue, e.g. 17-C-98 (Cork, 1998). The characters are white on a reflective green background.

69KB69   CHAPTER   

EIGHT

Military Vehicle Registrations

1903-1949

During the first half of the twentieth century there were various kinds of registration marks for military (Royal Navy, Royal Air Force and Army) vehicles. Initially, such vehicles carried normal civilian numberplates but sometimes had other serial numbers painted on their sides. After the outbreak of World War I in 1914 several different numbering techniques were used but in the latter half of 1918 a standardised scheme was introduced for War Department vehicles which were issued with marks consisting of a number followed by an identifying letter (B for Army vehicles, C for Royal Air Force vehicles, etc.) in yellow on a black (or dark) background.

In 1920, in accordance with the Roads Act of that year, military vehicles were once again issued with civilian marks. The responsibility for such registrations was given to Middlesex County Council who allocated blocks of their two-letter series (e.g. some of MH), then three-letter series (e.g. all of JME) to the War Department. After the outbreak of World War II in 1939, civilian registration of military vehicles ceased but when the war was over some vehicles which had originally carried civilian marks reverted to their old Middlesex numbers if sold on to non-military owners. Also some of the marks which had belonged to pre-war armoured vehicles were reissued to completely new civilian vehicles.

From 1939 to 1949 special serial marks called War Department numbers were used by all three services. Royal Navy vehicles were issued with marks consisting of four digits followed by the letters RN (beginning at 0001 RN); Royal Air Force vehicle numbers were made up of the letters RAF followed by up to six digits (e.g. RAF 132412); and the Army used a different letter for each type of vehicle, followed by a serial number of up to seven digits (e.g. M5863200), as follows:-

A - ambulances
C - motorcycles
D - Dragons (tracked towing vehicles for artillery)
E - engineering and earthmoving vehicles
F - armoured cars
H - tractors
L - heavy trucks
M - cars and coaches

P - amphibians
R - Rota trailers (for flamethrower tanks)
S - SPMs (Self-propelled Mountings), i.e. tracked chassis for carrying guns
T - tanks
V - vans
X - trailers
Z - light trucks

Army numbers were usually painted on the sides of the vehicles.

1949 - 1992

A completely new registration system for all military vehicles was introduced by the Ministry of Defence in 1949. This system employed a six-character Equipment Registration Mark (ERM) which was made up of two digits (from 00 to 99) followed by two letters followed by two digits (from 00 to 99), e.g. 06 RD 97. The middle letters related to the type of vehicle and/or the service to which the mark was issued, the Royal Navy using almost exclusively RN and the Royal Air Force using AA to AY (but excluding AI). The Army issued letter pairs beginning with BA and progressing to HZ, in addition to other combinations used for special categories such as XA to XK for vehicles commissioned in Germany, RA to RH for rebuilt pre-1949 vehicles, LV for leased vehicles, etc.

All older vehicles still in service were renumbered with the new-style marks except those operated by the Royal Navy which continued to carry wartime numbers until they were withdrawn. Also, unlike the other services, the Royal Navy recycled its ERMs, using those from discontinued vehicles to register new ones. Royal Navy trailers carried numbers of five digits followed by RN (a system still in use).

In 1980 the Army was given responsibility for buying most of the vehicles for all three services and issued a common ERM from the same series. The only exceptions were items of specialist Royal Navy and

Royal Air Force equipment which were issued with RN and AY marks respectively. This system was then superseded in 1982 by the implementation of series KA to KL, e.g. 14 KB 77, which was issued sequentially, the letters not relating to the vehicle type.

A list of ERM codes is shown on pages 89 to 91.

1993 Onwards

Since their inception in 1949, ERMs had been allocated manually but in 1993 a new computerised asset tracking system known as MERLIN was introduced which automatically generates new ERMs and then tracks them. These new-style marks reverse the previous pattern, consisting of two letters followed by two digits followed by two letters. The series started at AA 00 AA with numbers issued in sequence up to AA 99 AA. This was followed by AB 00 AA to AB 99 AA. Once all the prefix letters have been used with ending AA, i.e. after ZZ 99 AA, the series will start again at the beginning but using the suffix AB, i.e. AA 00 AB. These marks have not been adopted by the Royal Navy which continues to use two digits, RN, two digits.

Many military vehicles have numberplates with white characters on a black background but some which are used for non-tactical purposes (and therefore not requiring camouflage) such as cars, buses, etc., have reflective civilian-type plates. Also, since 1988, many passenger-carrying military vehicles, although issued with ERMs, have displayed ordinary civilian registration marks for security reasons.

Military marks in the Republic of Ireland are issued in Dublin and are of the normal type, e.g. 01-D-13501, but with white characters on a black background.

00 TG 07 (Army)

44   *(continued on page 57)*

Her Majesty the Queen's official cars do not carry registration plates.

115 D 103 (Diplomatic)
Official car, Republic of Benin

907 X 383   Cars belonging to staff of international organisations have diplomatic registration marks beginning with figure 9.

1 PY   HE The Paraguayan Ambassador, Embassy of Paraguay

SY 0
(Midlothian).
Provost's car,
Midlothian.

1 ABC (Leicester, 1960),
ABC 1 (Leicester, 1936).
Lord Mayor's cars,
Leicester.

J8 SAB (DVLA Select).
Mayor's car, Shrewsbury &
Atcham.

LBB 1L (Newcastle upon Tyne, 1972).
Mayor's car, London Borough of Bromley.

HG 1 (Burnley, 1930).
Mayor's car, Burnley.

GVU 1V
(Manchester, 1979).
Mayor's car, Chesterfield.

1 CFJ (Exeter, 1960).
Mayor's car, Exeter.

74 D 898 (Dublin). New-format
mark on older car with old-style plates.

660-BZF (Cork, 1986)

98-TS-513 (Tipperary, South
Riding, 1998)

93-WW-3008 (Co Wicklow, 1993)

DE-663 (Co Cavan) Trailer

97-D-3905 (Dublin, 1997)
Military

89-L-916 (Limerick City, 1989)

103 DZM (Co Galway, 1985)
Reflective plates (white front, red rear) were optional from 1969 to 1986.

HDI 869 (Co Roscommon, 1970)

ZV 6026 (Dublin) The ZV series is issued for vehicles aged 30 years or more if an 'old-style' mark is preferred.

01-D-19220 (Dublin, 2001)

ZZ 92486 The ZZ series is used for temporarily imported vehicles.

45748 (Guernsey)

J 91617 (Jersey) Hire car.

AY 999 (Alderney)

JSY 1 (Jersey)
Since 1999, numbers from a completely new series JSY 1 - JSY 999 have been available at auction. Registration number auctions are held once a year on behalf of the States of Jersey government.

55 (Guernsey) Cherished

Attractive Guernsey numbers, known as 'special' marks, are offered for sale from time to time at public auctions. Special marks include all those with fewer than five digits, and certain distinctive five-digit numbers, e.g. recently auctioned 55500, 70007, etc.

15179 (Guernsey)

AY 734 (Alderney)

J 12168 (Jersey)

MAN-3797
(1983, cherished)

25 RMN
(1969, cherished)

TMN-54
(1954, cherished)

6811-MAN
(1986, cherished)

FMN-782-C (2000)
with name of island
in Manx

Isle of Man prefixes and suffixes are not
'year-letters' as in Great Britain.

MAN 735L (1976, cherished)
CMN 86H (1992) with oval
GBM sticker
8008 MN (1963, cherished)

333 OMN (1969, cherished)

EMN-524-U (2000)
U 194 MAN (1982)
Unlike Great Britain, the Isle of Man includes suffix letter U. It also issued prefixes O and U.

BM 8752 (Bedfordshire, 1920). BM numbers, standing for Bentley Motors, were specially obtained by the makers for their three experimental models (number 2 shown here).

YN 3 (London, 1926)

S 7777 (Edinburgh, c.1919)   **ER 10** (Cambridgeshire, 1922)

H 21 (Middlesex, 1903)

AJ 20
(North Riding of Yorkshire, 1903)

JCB 968

(Blackburn, 1958)
One of almost a hundred
JCB plates, including
JCB 1, on the fleet of
J C Bamford Excavators
Ltd.

N1 PPY (DVLA Classic, 1996)
On a taxi belonging to a North Yorkshire
company - appropriate as company name
and local mark PY.

M1 GHT
(DVLA Classic, 1995)

IRL 1
(Special issue, 1958)
Originally the
mark (and car) of the
Irish ambassador in
London. Now
preserved by an
enthusiast.

AT02 HAT (DVLA Select, 2002)
Specially requested new-format marks can be obtained from DVLA - in this case a husband's and wife's initials.

Marks with the same final letter in both groups (e.g. RY51 SJY) are 'Select' and not issued in the normal sequence.

A1 BOG (DVLA Select)
Formerly omitted as an unsuitable combination, BOG has become available in the past few years. Notable examples are BOG 1 and BOG 1E sold at 'Classic' auctions.

SEP 1A (DVLA Classic, 1992)

1 SW (DVLA Classic, 1993)

NINE

How to Obtain a Cherished Number

Cherished Numbers

Numberplates themselves are almost worthless, except to people who collect them. When you acquire a cherished (or personalised) number you are obtaining the right to register your vehicle with that number. The number has to appear on the vehicle, the vehicle's registration document (logbook), the tax disc, the insurance certificate and, if the vehicle is of testable age, the test certificate.

Unless you buy a cherished number at the same time as a brand new car, the number has to undergo a cherished transfer from one vehicle to another (see page 60). If you buy from DVLA, DVLNI or a dealer, the transfer is usually done for you.

Registration marks in the United Kingdom can be transferred only between types of vehicle which are subject to annual testing, such as the so-called MOT test or HGV test. Several categories are therefore not eligible for cherished transfer including tractors, traction engines and electrically-propelled vehicles. Also it is necessary for both the donor vehicle and the recipient (receiving) vehicle to be registered on the DVLA or DVLNI computer and to have valid Vehicle Registration Documents (V5).

It is very important to note that a mark cannot be used on a vehicle if the mark makes the vehicle look newer than it really is. For example, N4 XTV could be used on an N prefix or later vehicle (1 August 1995 onwards, see page 75) but not on an earlier vehicle; TC51 BMK could be used on a 51 or later vehicle (1 September 2001 onwards) but not on an earlier vehicle. A number without a year identifier can be used on a vehicle of any age.

Dealers

One way of obtaining a cherished number is by consulting a dealer but it is a good idea first to read the latest issue of 'Exchange & Mart'. This newspaper contains many dealers' advertisements which display selections of available numbers and also usually quote websites which, if you have access to the internet, can then be visited.

Make sure that any dealer you consult is a member of either (or both of) the Cherished Numbers Dealers Association (CNDA, 201 Great Portland Street, LONDON W1N 6AB. Helpline 01788 538301) or the Institute of Registration Agents and Dealers (MIRAD, PO Box 333, SOUTHPORT, PR9 7GW. Tel: 07703 456789. www.mirad.co.uk).

Many dealers have access to vast lists of available numbers and it is worth phoning, writing or using the internet to give the dealer an idea of the kind of number you would like, such as your initials, with or without year letter, a particular sequence of numerals, etc.

Once you have made your choice the dealer will normally complete all the necessary documents and apply to transfer the number to your vehicle. Transfer costs may or may not be included in the dealer's price so it is sensible to find out the total cost before proceeding.

Private Buying

Another way of obtaining a number is to buy it privately. Numbers are advertised for private sale in newspapers such as Exchange & Mart and Sunday Times and in motoring magazines. It is also possible simply to spot an interesting number on an old car or motorcycle and ask the owner if he or she is willing to sell. Note, however, that the owner of a veteran, vintage or classic vehicle will not usually wish to separate the vehicle from its registration number as this can detract from the vehicle's value and authenticity.

When buying privately you usually have to complete your own transfer documents (see below). Be quite sure that the registration number is certain to be transferred to you before you make any payment. Perhaps it is stating the obvious, but do remember that there is no guaranteee that someone you do not know will deal honestly. Similarly, when selling a vehicle but keeping its registration mark, make certain that you have organised the transfer of the mark <u>before</u> you part with the vehicle or its documents. Valuable marks have been lost by not taking this precaution. If in doubt, consult a solicitor.

DVLA Auctions (Classic Collection and Custom Marks)

If you are interested in bidding for a cherished number in an auction, and are willing to pay £1000 or more, find out from DVLA when and where their next Classic Collection auction is to be held. These auctions take place approximately every three months at various places in Great Britain. The numbers on offer have never previously been issued and are taken by DVLA from hitherto unused series – for example 3 CP, 1 REX, HAG 1S. Many of these numbers do not have year letters.

Other registration numbers known as Custom Marks are also offered from time to time. These are sold at auction like the Classic Collection but they are deemed not 'universally attractive' and are therefore less expensive. DVLA will often put a particular number into one of their Classic or Custom sales if requested to do so by a member of the public.

DVLA auctions are advertised in newspapers and magazines and on the internet (www.dvla-som.co.uk), and catalogues and lists can be obtained before the sales take place. Bidding may be done in person or by telephone, post or internet. It is worth noting that prices are subject to a buyer's premium and VAT which are added on afterwards. Further information may be obtained by writing to Sale of Marks Marketing Team, DVLA, SWANSEA SA99 1DN.

DVLA Select Registrations

In addition to the Classic Collection and Custom Marks sold at auction, DVLA offers a range of comparatively less expensive 'Select Registrations' which can be bought by applying direct to DVLA by telephone or internet. These numbers can be either of two types. The 'old style' registrations (costing from £250 each) consist of a prefix letter followed by numerals (either from 1 to 20 or 'distinctive' such as 100, 555, etc.) and three letters, e.g. N99 ARB. Note, however, that the last three letters must not contain I, Q or Z and the prefix must not be I, Q, U or Z. Often the buyer can obtain the exact registration of his or her choice, provided that it has not already been sold.

The 'new format' registrations (from £499 each) consist of two letters (but not I, Q or Z) followed by two digits corresponding with the half-year of issue, and three letters (but not I or Q), e.g. JR52 PGR.

To find out whether your choice of Select registration is available, visit the DVLA website (www.dvla-som.co.uk) or ring 0870 6000 142.

DVLNI Auctions

DVLNI (Northern Ireland) also holds auctions of numbers. All these numbers contain either the letter I or the letter Z (or both) and none of them has a year letter. Details of forthcoming auctions and registration numbers offered for tender can be obtained from Wilsons Auctions Ltd., 22 Mallusk Road, NEWTOWNABBEY BT36 4PP (telephone 028 9034 2626), or from their website (www.wilsonsauctions.com).

Transfer Documents

If you wish to transfer a number yourself, either from a previous owner's car to yours, or your old car to a newer one, you should apply to your DVLA Local Office for an application form V317. This form contains all the information you need to know about the transfer of your number. An assignment fee of £80 must be paid to complete the transfer.

Numberplates

Unless your garage or local car showroom is obtaining your cherished number for you it is usually your responsibility to have the actual numberplates made. These must be reflective white (front) and reflective yellow (rear) except if the vehicle which is receiving the number was manufactured before 1 January 1973 in which case you can, if you wish, use black plates with white or silver characters.

Make sure that the letters and numerals on the plates are spaced correctly as it is illegal to use incorrect spacing. The numberplate supplier (car showroom, garage or car accessory shop) will advise you on this. Plates with the new Great Britain format (from 1 September 2001 onwards) must have characters of the correct font (typeface). These are shown on page 25.

Retention Certificates

It is possible to keep a registration mark without putting it on a vehicle. You can apply to DVLA on form V778/1, available from your DVLA Local Office. On payment of £80 assignment fee (for when the mark is eventually put on a vehicle) and £25 retention fee, you will be sent a Retention Certificate (V778) which shows that you are the keeper (the grantee) of the number.

4 IW and 1 IW (Co Derry, 1962). Cherished.

The certificate lasts for one year, after which it can be renewed for further years at a cost of £25 a year. Although a reminder is normally sent from DVLA shortly before renewal is due, it is your responsibility to make sure the retention is kept going. Failure to renew means that the mark will become void, i.e. you will lose it and it will disappear permanently from the DVLA records.

Reviving an Old Registration Mark

A vehicle whose registration mark has not been entered on the DVLA computer, i.e. a vehicle which has never had a V5 registration document, can still be registered under its original mark if sufficient evidence can be presented to DVLA that the mark genuinely belongs to the vehicle. This concession is for the benefit of enthusiasts who perhaps find a derelict car and wish to restore it to its original condition. In such a case it is necessary to seek the help of a specialist society, such as an owners' club, and it is worth noting that a revived mark of this kind cannot be transferred to another vehicle. Your DVLA Local Office will provide you with all the information required. It is not possible to revive a mark simply by owning an old registration document or 'log book'. The original vehicle must still exist.

Channel Islands and Isle of Man

In Jersey a cherished registration mark may be transferred from vehicle to vehicle, or put on retention for up to six months, for a fee of £62.00. It is also possible to bid at auction for registration marks in the series JSY 1-999 (and sometimes low numbers in the J series). Auctions are held annually on behalf of the States of Jersey by H.W. Maillard & Son, 34 Great Union Road, St Helier, JERSEY JE2 3YA (telephone 01534 737294).

Guernsey registration marks may be transferred or exchanged for a fee of £55.00. This fee is also payable for reserving an 'ordinary' five-digit mark. A mark can be put on retention for a maximum of two years for a fee of £55.00 a year. 'Special' marks such as palindromes, e.g. 45754, consecutives, e.g.34567, double-doubles, e.g.33188 or two-, three- and four-digit marks are available from time to time at public auctions or by tender. Auctions are held on behalf of the States of Guernsey (and some private clients) by Martel Maides, 40 Cornet Street, St Peter Port, GUERNSEY GY1 1LF (telephone 01481 722700).

Alderney marks may be transferred or retained for a fee of £27.50.

Cherished marks in the Isle of Man may be transferred for a fee of £60.00 and a mark can be put on retention at a cost of £60.00 for the first year and then £10.00 plus VAT for each ensuing year.

Republic of Ireland Reservations

In the Republic of Ireland it is not possible to cherish a registration mark (i.e. transfer it from vehicle to vehicle) but a particular mark from the coming year's sequence can be reserved in advance for a new vehicle on payment of €315. The only marks not available are the first number issued each year in Cork, Dublin, Limerick City and Waterford City (e.g. for 2003 the marks 03-C-1, 03-D-1, 03-L-1 and 03-W-1) as these are reserved for mayoral or lord-mayoral cars.

Application for a reserved mark should be made, on or after 1 November preceding the year of registration, to a Vehicle Registration Office or the Central Vehicle Office (for addresses see pages 96 and 97). Information is also available on the Revenue website (www.revenue.ie).

INDEX MARKS - 1903 TO AUGUST 2001

This list gives one-letter and two-letter index marks with issuing authorities. In a three-letter mark, example FAR 202, the last two letters identify the authority. In this example the letters are AR, indicating that the mark was originally issued by Hertfordshire County Council.

NOTE, however, that many 'cherished' marks have been specially 'created' by DVLA and have not been issued in the normal way.

Left to right:
Index mark.
Original registering council (B = County Borough or Large Burgh council. All others are County Council).
Date of first issue.
Local Vehicle Licensing Office from 1 October 1974 onwards (County or County Borough in the Republic of Ireland).

	Original	*1974 onwards*		*Original*	*1974 onwards*
A	London, 1904		BM	Bedfordshire, 1904	Luton
AA	Hampshire, 1903	Salisbury +	BN	Bolton B, 1904	Bolton +
AB	Worcestershire, 1904	Worcester	BO	Cardiff B, 1904	Cardiff
AC	Warwickshire, 1903	Coventry +	BP	West Sussex, 1904	Portsmouth
AD	Gloucestershire, 1903	Gloucester +	BR	Sunderland B, 1903	Durham +
AE	Bristol B, 1904	Bristol	BS	Orkney, 1903	Kirkwall +
AF	Cornwall, 1903	Truro	BT	Yorkshire (E.Riding), 1903	York +
AG	Ayrshire, 1925	Hull +	BU	Oldham B, 1903	Manchester
AH	Norfolk, 1904	Norwich	BV	Blackburn B, 1930	Preston
AI	Meath, 1903	Meath (until 1986)	BW	Oxfordshire, 1903	Oxford
AJ	Yorkshire (N.Riding), 1903	Middlesbrough +	BX	Carmarthenshire, 1903	Haverfordwest +
AK	Bradford B, 1903	Sheffield	BY	Croydon B, 1903	London (North West) +
AL	Nottinghamshire, 1903	Nottingham	BZ	Down, 1930	Downpatrick
AM	Wiltshire, 1903	Swindon +			
AN	West Ham, 1904	Reading	C	Yorkshire (W.Riding), 1904	
	MAN used by Isle of Man		CA	Denbighshire, 1904	Chester
AO	Cumberland, 1904	Carlisle	CB	Blackburn B, 1904	Bolton +
AP	East Sussex, 1903	Brighton	CC	Caernarvonshire, 1904	Bangor
AR	Hertfordshire, 1903	Chelmsford	CD	Brighton B, 1904	Brighton
AS	Nairnshire, 1903	Inverness	CE	Cambridgeshire, 1904	Cambridge +
AT	Kingston-upon-Hull B, 1904	Hull +	CF	West Suffolk, 1921	Reading
AU	Nottingham B, 1903	Nottingham	CG	Hampshire, 1931	Salisbury +
AV	Aberdeenshire, 1926	Peterborough	CH	Derby B, 1903	Nottingham
AW	Shropshire, 1903	Shrewsbury	CI	Laois, 1903	Laois (until 1986)
AX	Monmouthshire, 1904	Cardiff		*(formerly Queen's County)*	
AY	Leicestershire, 1903	Leicester +	CJ	Herefordshire, 1904	Hereford +
AZ	Belfast B, 1928	Belfast	CK	Preston B, 1904	Preston
			CL	Norwich B, 1904	Norwich
B	Lancashire, 1903		CM	Birkenhead B, 1904	Liverpool +
BA	Salford B, 1903	Manchester	CN	Gateshead B, 1903	Newcastle upon Tyne
BB	Newcastle upon Tyne B, 1904	Newcastle upon Tyne	CO	Plymouth B, 1904	Plymouth +
BC	Leicester B, 1904	Leicester +	CP	Halifax B, 1903	Huddersfield +
BD	Northamptonshire, 1903	Northampton	CR	Southampton B, 1903	Portsmouth
BE	Lincolnshire (Lindsey), 1903	Grimsby +	CS	Ayrshire, 1934	Ayr +
BF	Dorset, 1903	Stoke-on-Trent +	CT	Lincolnshire (Kesteven), 1903	Boston +
	BF 1 162 issued but later		CU	South Shields B, 1904	Newcastle upon Tyne
	withdrawn. Re-allocated to		CV	Cornwall, 1929	Truro
	Staffordshire in 1960 ¶		CW	Burnley B, 1904	Preston
BG	Birkenhead B, 1931	Liverpool +	CX	Huddersfield B, 1903	Huddersfield +
BH	Buckinghamshire, 1903	Luton	CY	Swansea B, 1903	Swansea
BI	Monaghan, 1903	Monaghan (until 1986)		*SCY transferred to*	
BJ	East Suffolk, 1904	Ipswich		*Cornwall in 1971 for use*	
BK	Portsmouth B, 1903	Portsmouth		*in Isles of Scilly*	
BL	Berkshire, 1904	Reading	CZ	Belfast B, 1932	Belfast

+ Office now closed, relocated or renamed. See page 69.   ¶ Three-letter marks only, starting at CBF.

Index Marks 1903-2001

	Original	1974 onwards		Original	1974 onwards
D	Kent, 1903		FD	Dudley B, 1903	Dudley +
DA	Wolverhampton B, 1903	Birmingham	FE	Lincoln B, 1904	Lincoln
DB	Stockport B, 1903	Manchester	FF	Merionethshire, 1904	Aberystwyth +
DC	Middlesbrough B, 1903	Middlesbrough +	FG	Fife, 1925	Brighton
DD	Gloucestershire, 1921	Gloucester +	FH	Gloucester B, 1903	Gloucester +
DE	Pembrokeshire, 1903	Haverfordwest +	FI	Tipperary (N.Riding), 1903	Tipperary N(until 1986)
DF	Northampton B, 1903	Gloucester +	FJ	Exeter B, 1904	Exeter
	Withdrawn soon after issue.		FK	Worcester B, 1903	Dudley +
	Reissued to Gloucestershire 1926.		FL	Soke of Peterborough, 1903	Peterborough
DG	Gloucestershire, 1930	Gloucester +	FM	Chester B, 1904	Chester
DH	Walsall B, 1904	Dudley +	FN	Canterbury B, 1904	Canterbury +
DI	Roscommon, 1903	Roscommon(until 1986)	FO	Radnorshire, 1903	Hereford +
DJ	St Helens B, 1903	Warrington +	FP	Rutland, 1903	Leicester +
DK	Rochdale B, 1903	Bolton +	FR	Blackpool B, 1904	Preston
DL	Isle of Wight, 1903	Newport (IoW) +	FS	Edinburgh B, 1931	Edinburgh
DM	Flintshire, 1903	Chester	FT	Tynemouth B, 1904	Newcastle upon Tyne
DN	York B, 1903	York +	FU	Lincolnshire (Lindsey), 1922	Grimsby +
DO	Lincolnshire (Holland), 1903	Boston +	FV	Blackpool B, 1929	Preston
DP	Reading B, 1903	Reading	FW	Lincolnshire (Lindsey), 1929	Lincoln
DR	Devonport B, 1904	Plymouth +	FX	Dorset, 1904	Bournemouth
	Up to DR 268. Then		FY	Southport B, 1905	Liverpool +
	transferred to Plymouth		FZ	Belfast B, 1938	Belfast
	in 1915.				
DS	Peeblesshire, 1903	Glasgow	G	Glasgow B, 1903	
DT	Doncaster B, 1927	Sheffield	GA	Glasgow B, 1921	Glasgow
DU	Coventry B, 1903	Coventry +	GB	Glasgow B, 1922	Glasgow
DV	Devon, 1929	Exeter	GC	London, 1929	London SW +
DW	Newport (Wales) B, 1904	Cardiff	GD	Glasgow B, 1925	Glasgow
DX	Ipswich B, 1904	Ipswich	GE	Glasgow B, 1928	Glasgow
DY	Hastings B, 1904	Hastings +	GF	London, 1930	London SW +
DZ	Antrim, 1932	Ballymena	GG	Glasgow, 1930	Glasgow
			GH	London, 1930	London SW +
E	Staffordshire, 1904		GI	Tipperary (S.Riding), 1985 ¶	Tipperary S(until 1986)
EA	West Bromwich B, 1904	Dudley +	GJ	London, 1930	London SW +
EB	Isle of Ely, 1903	Cambridge +	GK	London, 1930	London SW +
EC	Westmorland, 1903	Kendal +	GL	Bath B, 1932	Truro
ED	Warrington B, 1903	Warrington +	GM	Motherwell & Wishaw B, 1920	Reading
EE	Grimsby B, 1904	Grimsby +	GN	London, 1931	London SW +
EF	West Hartlepool B, 1903	Middlesbrough +	GO	London, 1931	London SW +
EG	Soke of Peterborough, 1931	Peterborough	GP	London, 1931	London SW +
EH	Hanley B, 1904	Stoke-on-Trent +	GR	Sunderland B, 1933	Durham +
	Became part of		GS	Perthshire, 1928	Luton
	Stoke-on-Trent in 1910.		GT	London, 1931	London SW +
EI	Sligo, 1903	Sligo (until 1986)	GU	London, 1929	London SE +
EJ	Cardiganshire, 1904	Aberystwyth +	GV	West Suffolk, 1930	Ipswich
EK	Wigan B, 1904	Warrington +	GW	London, 1931	London SE +
EL	Bournemouth B, 1903	Bournemouth	GX	London, 1932	London SE +
EM	Bootle B, 1903	Liverpool +	GY	London, 1932	London SE+
EN	Bury B, 1903	Bolton +	GZ	Belfast B, 1942	Belfast
EO	Barrow-in-Furness B, 1904	Barrow-in-Furness +			
EP	Montgomeryshire, 1903	Swansea	H	Middlesex, 1903	
ER	Cambridgeshire, 1922	Cambridge +	HA	Smethwick B, 1907	Dudley +
ES	Perthshire, 1903	Dundee	HB	Merthyr Tydfil B, 1908	Cardiff
ET	Rotherham B, 1903	Sheffield	HC	Eastbourne B, 1911	Hastings +
EU	Breconshire, 1903	Bristol	HD	Dewsbury B, 1913	Huddersfield +
EV	Essex, 1931	Chelmsford	HE	Barnsley B, 1913	Sheffield
EW	Huntingdonshire, 1903	Peterborough	HF	Wallasey B, 1913	Liverpool +
EX	Great Yarmouth B, 1904	Norwich	HG	Burnley B, 1930	Preston
EY	Anglesey, 1903	Bangor	HH	Carlisle B, 1914	Carlisle
EZ	Belfast B, 1935	Belfast	HI	Tipperary (S.Riding), 1903	Tipperary S(until 1986)
			HJ	Southend-on-Sea, 1914	Chelmsford
F	Essex, 1904		HK	Essex, 1915	Chelmsford
FA	Burton-on-Trent B, 1903	Stoke-on-Trent +	HL	Wakefield B, 1915	Sheffield
FB	Bath B, 1903	Bristol	HM	East Ham B, 1916	London Central +
FC	Oxford B, 1903	Oxford	HN	Darlington B, 1921	Middlesbrough +

+ Office now closed, relocated or renamed. See page 69. ¶ Three-letter marks only, starting at AGI.

64

Original	1974 onwards	Original	1974 onwards
HO Hampshire, 1917	Salisbury +	**K** Liverpool B, 1903	
HP Coventry B, 1919	Coventry +	**KA** Liverpool B, 1925	Liverpool +
HR Wiltshire, 1919	Swindon +	**KB** Liverpool B, 1914	Liverpool +
HS Renfrewshire, 1903	Glasgow	**KC** Liverpool B, 1920	Liverpool +
HT Bristol B, 1920	Bristol	**KD** Liverpool B, 1927	Liverpool +
HU Bristol B, 1924	Bristol	**KE** Kent, 1920	Maidstone
HV East Ham B, 1930	London Central +	**KF** Liverpool B, 1930	Liverpool +
HW Bristol B, 1927	Bristol	**KG** Cardiff B, 1931	Cardiff
HX Middlesex, 1930	London Central +	**KH** Kingston-upon-Hull B, 1925	Hull +
HY Bristol B, 1930	Bristol	**KI** Waterford, 1904	Waterford (until 1986)
HZ Tyrone, 1944	Omagh	**KJ** Kent, 1931	Maidstone
		KK Kent, 1922	Maidstone
IA Antrim, 1903	Ballymena	**KL** Kent, 1924	Maidstone
IB Armagh, 1903	Armagh	**KM** Kent, 1925	Maidstone
IC Carlow, 1903	Carlow (until 1986)	**KN** Kent, 1917	Maidstone
ID Cavan, 1904	Cavan (until 1986)	**KO** Kent, 1927	Maidstone
IE Clare, 1903	Clare (until 1986)	**KP** Kent, 1928	Maidstone
IF Cork, 1903	Cork (until 1986)	**KR** Kent, 1929	Maidstone
IH Donegal, 1903	Donegal (until 1986)	**KS** Roxburghshire, 1903	Selkirk +
IJ Down, 1903	Downpatrick	**KT** Kent, 1913	Canterbury +
IK Dublin, 1903	Dublin (until 1986)	**KU** Bradford B, 1922	Sheffield
IL Fermanagh, 1904	Enniskillen	**KV** Coventry B, 1931	Coventry +
IM Galway, 1903	Galway (until 1986)	**KW** Bradford B, 1926	Sheffield
IN Kerry, 1903	Kerry (until 1986)	**KX** Buckinghamshire, 1928	Luton
IO Kildare, 1903	Kildare (until 1986)	**KY** Bradford B, 1931	Sheffield
IP Kilkenny, 1904	Kilkenny (until 1986)	**KZ** Antrim, 1947	Ballymena
IR Offaly, 1903	Offaly (until 1986)		
(formerly King's County)		**L** Glamorganshire, 1904	
IS Mayo, 1983 ¶	Mayo (until 1986)	**LA** London, 1910	London NW +
IT Leitrim, 1903	Leitrim (until 1986)	**LB** London, 1908	London NW +
IU Limerick, 1903	Limerick (until 1986)	**LC** London, 1905	London NW +
IV Limerick, 1982 ¶	Limerick (until 1986)	**LD** London, 1909	London NW +
IW Londonderry, 1903	Coleraine	**LE** London, 1911	London NW +
IX Longford, 1903	Longford (until 1986)	**LF** London, 1912	London NW +
IY Louth, 1903	Louth (until 1986)	**LG** Cheshire, 1928	Chester
IZ Mayo, 1904	Mayo (until 1986)	**LH** London, 1913	London NW +
		LI Westmeath, 1903	Westmeath (until 1986)
J Durham, 1903		**LJ** Bournemouth B, 1929	Bournemouth
JA Stockport B, 1929	Manchester	**LK** London, 1913	London NW +
JB Berkshire, 1932	Reading	**LL** London, 1914	London NW +
JC Caernarvonshire, 1931	Bangor	**LM** London, 1914	London NW +
JD West Ham B, 1929	London Central +	**LN** London, 1906	London NW +
JE Isle of Ely, 1933	Cambridge +	**LO** London, 1915	London NW +
JF Leicester B, 1930	Leicester +	**LP** London, 1915	London NW +
JG Canterbury B, 1929	Canterbury +	**LR** London, 1916	London NW +
JH Hertfordshire, 1931	Reading	**LS** Selkirkshire, 1903	Stirling +
JI Tyrone, 1903	Omagh	**LT** London, 1918	London NW +
JJ London, 1932	Canterbury +	**LU** London, 1919	London NW +
JK Eastbourne B, 1928	Hastings +	**LV** Liverpool B, 1932	Liverpool +
JL Lincolnshire (Holland), 1932	Boston +	**LW** London, 1919	London NW +
JM Westmorland, 1931	Reading	**LX** London, 1919	London NW +
JN Southend-on-Sea, 1930	Chelmsford	**LY** London, 1919	London NW +
JO Oxford B, 1930	Oxford	**LZ** Armagh, 1947	Armagh
JP Wigan B, 1934	Warrington +		
JR Northumberland, 1932	Newcastle upon Tyne	**M** Cheshire, 1903	
J3 Ross & Cromarty, 1903	Stornoway +	**MA** Cheshire, 1919	Chester
JT Dorset, 1933	Bournemouth	**MB** Cheshire, 1922	Chester
JU Leicestershire, 1931	Leicester +	**MC** Middlesex, 1917	London NE +
JV Grimsby B, 1930	Grimsby +	**MD** Middlesex, 1920	London NE +
JW Wolverhampton B, 1931	Birmingham	**ME** Middlesex, 1921	London NE +
JX Halifax B, 1932	Huddersfield +	**MF** Middlesex, 1923	London NE +
JY Plymouth, 1932	Plymouth		**MG** Middlesex, 1930	London NE +
JZ Down, 1946	Downpatrick	**MH** Middlesex, 1924	London NE +

+ Office now closed, relocated or renamed. See page 69.
¶ Three-letter marks only, starting at AIS and AIV.

Original	1974 onwards	Original	1974 onwards
MI Wexford, 1904	Wexford (until 1986)	**OS** Wigtownshire, 1904	Stranraer +
MJ Bedfordshire, 1932	Luton	**OT** Hampshire, 1926	Portsmouth
MK Middlesex, 1925	London NE +	**OU** Hampshire, 1928	Bristol
ML Middlesex, 1926	London NE +	**OV** Birmingham B, 1931	Birmingham
MM Middlesex, 1926	London NE +	**OW** Southampton B, 1931	Portsmouth
MN Isle of Man, 1906	Isle of Man	**OX** Birmingham B, 1927	Birmingham
MO Berkshire, 1922	Reading	**OY** Croydon B, 1931	London NW +
MP Middlesex, 1927	London NE +	**OZ** Belfast B, 1950	Belfast
MR Wiltshire, 1924	Swindon +		
MS Stirlingshire, 1903	Stirling +	**P** Surrey, 1904	
MT Middlesex, 1928	London NE +	**PA** Surrey, 1913	Guildford +
MU Middlesex, 1929	London NE +	**PB** Surrey, 1919	Guildford +
MV Middlesex, 1931	London SE +	**PC** Surrey, 1921	Guildford +
MW Wiltshire, 1927	Swindon +	**PD** Surrey, 1923	Guildford +
MX Middlesex, 1912	London SE +	**PE** Surrey, 1924	Guildford +
MY Middlesex, 1929	London SE +	**PF** Surrey, 1926	Guildford +
MZ Belfast B, 1947	Belfast	**PG** Surrey, 1929	Guildford +
		PH Surrey, 1927	Guildford +
N Manchester B, 1904		**PI** Cork B, 1903	Cork B (until 1986)
NA Manchester B, 1913	Manchester	**PJ** Surrey, 1931	Guildford +
NB Manchester B, 1919	Manchester	**PK** Surrey, 1928	Guildford +
NC Manchester B, 1920	Manchester	**PL** Surrey, 1930	Guildford +
ND Manchester B, 1923	Manchester	**PM** East Sussex, 1922	Guildford +
NE Manchester B, 1925	Manchester	**PN** East Sussex, 1927	Brighton
NF Manchester B, 1926	Manchester	**PO** West Sussex, 1929	Portsmouth
NG Norfolk, 1930	Norwich	*GPO issued by London CC,*	
NH Northampton B, 1904	Northampton	*see page 10.*	
NI Wicklow, 1904	Wicklow (until 1986)	**PP** Buckinghamshire, 1923	Luton
QNI issued in Northern		**PR** Dorset, 1923	Bournemouth
Ireland, see page 37.		**PS** Shetland, 1904	Lerwick +
NJ East Sussex, 1932	Brighton	**PT** Durham, 1922	Durham +
NK Hertfordshire, 1921	Luton	**PU** Essex, 1923	Chelmsford
NL Northumberland, 1921	Newcastle upon Tyne	**PV** Ipswich B, 1932	Ipswich
NM Bedfordshire, 1920	Luton	**PW** Norfolk, 1923	Norwich
NN Nottinghamshire, 1921	Nottingham	**PX** West Sussex, 1923	Portsmouth
NO Essex, 1921	Chelmsford	**PY** Yorkshire (N.Riding), 1923	Middlesbrough +
NP Worcestershire, 1921	Worcester	**PZ** Belfast B, 1953	Belfast
NR Leicestershire, 1921	Leicester +		
NS Sutherland, 1904	Glasgow	**QA** London	London Central +
NT Shropshire, 1921	Shrewsbury	**QB** London	London Central +
NU Derbyshire, 1923	Nottingham	**QC** London	London Central +
NV Northamptonshire, 1931	Northampton	**QD** London	London Central +
NW Leeds B, 1921	Leeds	**QE** London	London Central +
NX Warwickshire, 1921	Dudley +	**QF** London	London Central +
NY Glamorganshire, 1921	Cardiff	**QG** London *All Q series*	London Central +
NZ Londonderry, 1949	Coleraine	**QH** London *for issue*	London Central +
		QJ London *to temporarily*	London Central +
O Birmingham B, 1904		**QK** London *imported vehicles.*	London Central +
OA Birmingham B, 1913	Birmingham	**QL** London *See page 37.*	London Central +
OB Birmingham B, 1915	Birmingham	**QM** London	London Central +
OC Birmingham B, 1933	Birmingham	**QN** London	London Central +
OD Devon, 1931	Exeter	**QO** London	London Central +
OE Birmingham B, 1919	Birmingham	**QP** London	London Central +
OF Birmingham, 1929	Birmingham	**QQ** London	London Central +
OG Birmingham, 1930	Birmingham	**QR** London	London Central +
OH Birmingham B, 1920	Birmingham	**QS** London	London Central +
OI Belfast B, 1904	Belfast	**QT** London	London Central +
OJ Birmingham B, 1932	Birmingham	**QU** London	London Central +
OK Birmingham B, 1922	Birmingham	**QV** London	London Central +
OL Birmingham B, 1923	Birmingham	**QW** London	London Central +
OM Birmingham B, 1924	Birmingham	**QX** London	London Central +
ON Birmingham B, 1925	Birmingham	**QY** London	London Central +
OO Essex, 1961	Chelmsford		
OP Birmingham B, 1926	Birmingham	**R** Derbyshire, 1903	
OR Hampshire, 1922	Portsmouth	**RA** Derbyshire, 1926	Nottingham

+ Office now closed, relocated or renamed. See page 69.

Original	1974 onwards	Original	1974 onwards
RB Derbyshire, 1929	Nottingham	**TH** Carmarthenshire, 1929	Swansea
RC Derby B, 1931	Nottingham	**TI** Limerick B, 1904	Limerick B (until 1986)
RD Reading B, 1928	Reading	**TJ** Lancashire, 1932	Liverpool +
RE Staffordshire, 1921	Stoke-on-Trent +	**TK** Dorset, 1927	Plymouth +
RF Staffordshire, 1924	Stoke-on-Trent +	**TL** Lincolnshire (Kesteven), 1928	Lincoln
RG Aberdeen B, 1928	Newcastle upon Tyne	**TM** Bedfordshire, 1927	Luton
RH Kingston-upon-Hull, 1930	Hull +	**TN** Newcastle upon Tyne B, 1925	Newcastle upon Tyne
RI Dublin B, 1903	Dublin (until 1986)	**TO** Nottingham B, 1924	Nottingham
RJ Salford B, 1931	Manchester	**TP** Portsmouth B, 1924	Portsmouth
RK Croydon B, 1922	London NW +	**TR** Southampton B, 1925	Portsmouth
RL Cornwall, 1924	Truro	**TS** Dundee B, 1904	Dundee
RM Cumberland, 1924	Carlisle	**TT** Devon, 1924	Exeter
RN Preston B, 1928	Preston	**TU** Cheshire, 1925	Chester
RO Hertfordshire, 1925	Luton	**TV** Nottingham B, 1929	Nottingham
RP Northamptonshire, 1924	Northampton	**TW** Essex, 1925	Chelmsford
RR Nottinghamshire, 1925	Nottingham	**TX** Glamorganshire, 1926	Cardiff
RS Aberdeen B, 1904	Aberdeen	**TY** Northumberland, 1925	Newcastle upon Tyne
RT East Suffolk, 1925	Ipswich	**TZ** Belfast B, 1954	Belfast
RU Bournemouth B, 1924	Bournemouth		
RV Portsmouth B, 1931	Portsmouth	**U** Leeds B, 1904	
RW Coventry B, 1924	Coventry +	**UA** Leeds B, 1927	Leeds
RX Berkshire, 1927	Reading	**UB** Leeds B, 1929	Leeds
RY Leicester B, 1925	Leicester +	**UC** London, 1928	London Central +
RZ Antrim, 1954	Ballymena	**UD** Oxfordshire, 1926	Oxford
		UE Warwickshire, 1925	Dudley +
S Edinburgh B, 1903		**UF** Brighton B, 1925	Brighton
SA Aberdeenshire, 1904	Aberdeen	**UG** Leeds B, 1932	Leeds
SB Argyllshire, 1904	Oban +	**UH** Cardiff B, 1925	Cardiff
SC Edinburgh B, 1927	Edinburgh	**UI** Londonderry B, 1904	Londonderry
SD Ayrshire, 1904	Ayr +	**UJ** Shropshire, 1932	Shrewsbury
SE Banffshire, 1904	Keith +	**UK** Wolverhampton B, 1925	Birmingham
SF Edinburgh B, 1924	Edinburgh	**UL** London, 1929	London Central +
SG Edinburgh B, 1920	Edinburgh	**UM** Leeds B, 1925	Leeds
SH Berwickshire, 1903	Selkirk +	**UN** Denbighshire, 1927	Barnstaple +
SI Dublin, 1986	Dublin (1986 only)	**UO** Devon, 1926	Barnstaple +
SJ Bute, 1904	Ayr +	**UP** Durham, 1927	Durham +
SK Caithness, 1903	Wick +	**UR** Hertfordshire, 1928	Luton
SL Clackmannanshire, 1903	Dundee	**US** Govan B, 1904	Glasgow
SM Dumfriesshire, 1903	Dumfries +	*Transferred to Glasgow 1912.*	
SN Dunbartonshire, 1903	Dundee	**UT** Leicestershire, 1927	Leicester +
USN not issued		**UU** London, 1929	London Central +
SO Moray, 1903	Aberdeen	**UV** London, 1929	London Central +
(formerly Elginshire)		**UW** London, 1929	London Central +
SP Fife, 1903	Dundee	**UX** Shropshire, 1927	Shrewsbury
SR Angus, 1904	Dundee	**UY** Worcestershire, 1927	Worcester
(formerly Forfarshire)		**UZ** Belfast B, 1955	Belfast
SS East Lothian, 1904	Aberdeen		
(formerly Haddingtonshire)		**V** Lanarkshire, 1904	
ST Invernessshire, 1904	Inverness	**VA** Lanarkshire, 1922	Cambridge +
SU Kincardineshire, 1904	Glasgow	**VB** Croydon B, 1927	Canterbury +
SV Kinrossshire, 1904	-	**VC** Coventry B, 1929	Coventry +
SW Kirkcudbrightshire, 1903	Dumfries +	**VD** Lanarkshire, 1930	Luton
SX West Lothian, 1904	Edinburgh	**VE** Cambridgeshire, 1928	Cambridge +
(formerly Linlithgowshire)		**VF** Norfolk, 1927	Norwich
SY Midlothian, 1903	-	**VG** Norwich B, 1927	Norwich
SZ Down, 1954	Downpatrick	**VH** Huddersfield B, 1927	Huddersfield +
		VJ Herefordshire, 1927	Hereford +
T Devon, 1904		**VK** Newcastle upon Tyne B, 1929	Newcastle upon Tyne
TA Devon, 1920	Exeter	**VL** Lincoln B, 1928	Lincoln
TB Lancashire, 1919	Warrington +	**VM** Manchester B, 1928	Manchester
TC Lancashire, 1922	Bristol	**VN** Yorkshire (N.Riding), 1929	Middlesbrough +
TD Lancashire, 1924	Bolton +	**VO** Nottinghamshire, 1928	Nottingham
TE Lancashire, 1927	Bolton +	**VP** Birmingham B, 1928	Birmingham
TF Lancashire, 1929	Reading	**VR** Manchester B, 1929	Manchester
TG Glamorganshire, 1930	Cardiff	**VS** Greenock B, 1903	Luton

+ Office now closed, relocated or renamed. See page 69.

Index Marks 1903-2001

	Original	1974 onwards		Original	1974 onwards
VT	Stoke-on-Trent B, 1927	Stoke-on-Trent +	XW	London, 1924	-
VU	Manchester B, 1930	Manchester	XX	London, 1925	-
VV	Northampton B, 1930	Northampton	XY	London, 1925	-
VW	Essex, 1927	Chelmsford	XZ	Armagh, 1957	Armagh
VX	Essex, 1929	Chelmsford			
VY	York B, 1928	York +	Y	Somerset, 1903	
VZ	Tyrone, 1956	Omagh	YA	Somerset, 1921	Taunton +
			YB	Somerset, 1924	Taunton +
W	Sheffield B, 1904		YC	Somerset, 1927	Taunton +
WA	Sheffield B, 1919	Sheffield	YD	Somerset, 1930	Taunton +
WB	Sheffield B, 1924	Sheffield	YE	London, 1927	London Central +
WC	Essex, 1962 ¶	Chelmsford	YF	London, 1927	London Central +
WD	Warwickshire, 1930	Dudley +	YG	Yorkshire (W.Riding), 1932	Leeds
WE	Sheffield B, 1927	Sheffield	YH	London, 1927	London Central +
WF	Yorkshire (E.Riding), 1926	Sheffield	YI	Dublin B, 1921	Dublin (until 1986)
WG	Stirlingshire, 1930	Sheffield	YJ	Dundee B, 1932	Brighton
WH	Bolton B, 1927	Bolton +	YK	London, 1925	London Central +
WI	Waterford B, 1903	Waterford B(until 1986)	YL	London, 1925	London Central +
WJ	Sheffield B, 1930	Sheffield	YM	London, 1925	London Central +
WK	Coventry B, 1926	Coventry +	YN	London, 1926	London Central +
WL	Oxford B, 1925	Oxford	YO	London, 1926	London Central +
WM	Southport B, 1927	Liverpool +	YP	London, 1926	London Central +
WN	Swansea B, 1927	Swansea	YR	London, 1926	London Central +
WO	Monmouthshire, 1927	Cardiff	YS	Partick B, 1904	Glasgow
WP	Worcestershire, 1931	Worcester		*Transferred to Glasgow 1912.*	
WR	Yorkshire (W.Riding), 1912	Leeds	YT	London, 1927	London Central +
WS	Leith B, 1903	Bristol	YU	London, 1927	London Central +
	Transferred to Edinburgh 1920.		YV	London, 1928	London Central +
			YW	London, 1928	London Central +
WT	Yorkshire (W.Riding), 1923	Leeds	YX	London, 1928	London Central +
WU	Yorkshire (W.Riding), 1925	Leeds	YY	London, 1932	London Central +
WV	Wiltshire, 1931	Brighton	YZ	Londonderry, 1957	Coleraine
WW	Yorkshire (W.Riding), 1927	Leeds			
WX	Yorkshire (W.Riding), 1929	Leeds	Z	Dublin, 1927	
WY	Yorkshire (W.Riding), 1921	Leeds	ZA	Dublin B, 1933	Dublin (until 1986)
WZ	Belfast B, 1957	Belfast	ZB	Cork, 1935	Cork (until 1986)
			ZC	Dublin B, 1937	Dublin (until 1986)
			ZD	Dublin B, 1940	Dublin (until 1986)
X	Northumberland, 1903		ZE	Dublin, 1940	Dublin (until 1986)
XA	London, 1920 (see page 21)	-	ZF	Cork B, 1946	Cork (until 1986)
XB	London, 1920 (see page 21)	-	ZG	Dublin Co & B, 1986	Dublin (1986 only)
XC	London, 1920 (see page 21)	-	ZH	Dublin B, 1947	Dublin (until 1986)
XD	London, 1920 (see page 21)	-	ZI	Dublin B, 1927	Dublin (until 1986)
XE	London, 1920 (see page 21)	-	ZJ	Dublin B, 1949	Dublin (until 1986)
XF	London, 1921 (see page 21)	-	ZK	Cork, 1949	Cork (until 1986)
XG	Middlesbrough B, 1929	-	ZL	Dublin B, 1950	Dublin (until 1986)
XH	London, 1921	-	ZM	Galway, 1950	Galway (until 1986)
XI	Belfast B, 1922	Belfast	ZN	Meath, 1951	Meath (until 1986)
XJ	Manchester B, 1932	-	ZO	Dublin Co & B, 1952	Dublin (until 1986)
XK	London, 1922	-	ZP	Donegal, 1952	Donegal (until 1986)
XL	London, 1922	-	ZR	Wexford, 1952	Wexford (until 1986)
XM	London, 1922	-	ZS	Dublin Co & B, 1986	Dublin (1986 only)
XN	London, 1923	-	ZT	Cork, 1953	Cork (until 1986)
XO	London, 1923	-	ZU	Dublin Co & B, 1953	Dublin (until 1986)
XP	London, 1923	Temporary export registrations (see page 37)	ZV	Dublin Co & B, 1985	Dublin (until 1986)
				AZV to YZV only.	
				ZV without prefix used, from	
XR	London, 1924	-		*1992, as 'age-related' marks*	
XS	Paisley B, 1904	London Central + RXS only. Used for some diplomats' cars.		*(see page 35).*	
			ZW	Kildare, 1953	Kildare (until 1986)
			ZX	Kerry, 1954	Kerry (until 1986)
XT	London, 1924	-	ZY	Louth, 1954	Louth (until 1986)
XU	London, 1924	-	ZZ	Dublin & other offices, 1926	For temporary imports
XV	London, 1928	-			

+ Office now closed, relocated or renamed. See page 69.
¶ Three-letter marks only, starting at BWC.

LVLOs/VROs CLOSED 1980 - 1997

Office	Date	Business transferred to
Aberystwyth	1981	Haverfordwest (until 1996) and Bangor
Ayr	1981	Glasgow
Barnstaple	1981	Exeter
Barrow-in-Furness	1981	Preston
Bolton	1981	Manchester
Boston	1981	Lincoln
Cambridge	1980	Peterborough
Canterbury	1981	Maidstone
Coventry	1997	Birmingham, Northampton, Nottingham, Oxford and Worcester
Dudley	1993	Birmingham
Dumfries	1981	Carlisle
Durham	1981	Newcastle upon Tyne
Gloucester	1997	Bristol and Worcester
Grimsby	1980	Lincoln
Guildford	1997	Portsmouth, Reading and Wimbledon
Hastings	1980	Brighton
Haverfordwest	1997	Swansea
Hereford	1981	Gloucester (until 1997)
Huddersfield	1994	Leeds
Keith	1981	Aberdeen
Kendal	1981	Preston
Kirkwall	1980	Inverness
Leicester	1996	Birmingham, Northampton, Nottingham and Peterborough
Lerwick	1980	Aberdeen
Liverpool	1996	Chester and Preston
London Central	1997	Wimbledon
London NE	1996	Chelmsford
Newport (Isle of Wight)	1981	Portsmouth
Oban	1980	Glasgow
Plymouth	1980	Exeter
Salisbury	1980	Bournemouth
Selkirk	1980	Edinburgh
At Newtown St Boswells until 1975		
Stirling	1981	Edinburgh
Stoke-on-Trent	1996	Birmingham and Shrewsbury
Stornoway	1980	Inverness
Stranraer	1981	Glasgow
Swindon	1997	Bristol
Taunton	1996	Bristol and Exeter
Warrington	1981	Liverpool (until 1996)
Wick	1981	Inverness
York	1980	Leeds

Hull VRO was relocated to Beverley in 1996.
London NW now known as Stanmore.
London SE now known as Sidcup.
London SW now known as Wimbledon.
Middlesbrough VRO was relocated to Stockton-on-Tees in 2000.

Authorities 1903-1974

This list gives details of licensing authorities in the United Kingdom (until 1974) and the Republic of Ireland. The original series of marks was subsequently modified or replaced by new systems incorporating year-letters (Great Britain in 1963-5) or year-numerals (Republic of Ireland in 1987). Northern Ireland has continued without year identifiers. Note that 'last normal marks' does not include subsequent marks issued as replacements in cherished transfers (see pages 33 to 35).

Authority	One- and two- letter marks in order of issue	First 3-letter mark with date of issue		Last normal mark before year identifiers	First 'year-identifier' mark with date of issue	
Aberdeen	RS, RG	ARG 1	12/38	WRS 322	ARG 1B	5/64
Aberdeenshire	SA, AV	AAV 1	1/38	YSA 981	AAV 1A	12/63
Anglesey	EY	AEY 1	6/51	PEY 112	AEY 1B	4/64
Angus	SR	ASR 1	6/36	8567 SR	ASR 1B	7/64
Antrim	IA, DZ, KZ, RZ	AIA 1	1/66	—	—	
Argyllshire	SB	ASB 1	5/54	NSB 99	ASB 1C	1/65
Armagh	IB, LZ, XZ	AIB 1	3/72	—	—	
Ayrshire	SD, AG, CS	AAG 1	5/39	YSD 259	AAG 1B	6/64
Banffshire	SE	ASE 1	5/56	HSE 900	ASE 1B	5/64
Barnsley	HE	AHE 1	3/45	6710 HE	AHE 1B	7/64
Barrow-in-Furness	EO	AEO 1	9/52	MEO 274	AEO 1B	9/64
Bath	FB, GL	AFB 1	6/47	OGL 960	AFB 1B	1/64
Bedfordshire	BM, NM, TM, MJ	ABM 1	3/36	65 RBM	ABM 1C	1/65
Belfast	OI, XI, AZ, CZ, EZ, FZ, GZ, MZ, OZ, PZ, TZ, UZ, WZ	AOI 1	4/69	—	—	
Berkshire	BL, MO, RX, JB	ABL 1	8/36	344 GBL	ABL 1B	2/64
Berwickshire	SH	ASH 1	11/52	KSH 638	ASH 1B	7/64
Birkenhead	CM, BG	ACM 1	1/48	SCM 966	ACM 1B	8/64
Birmingham	O, OA, OB, OE, OH, OK, OL, OM, ON, OP, OX, VP, OF, OG, OV, OJ, OC	AOA 1	3/34	555 NOJ	AOA 1B	8/64
Blackburn	CB, BV	ABV 1	8/39	SCB 950	ABV 1B	1/64
Blackpool	FR, FV	AFR 1	12/37	637 JFR	AFR 1B	6/64
Bolton	BN, WH	ABN 1	4/38	YWH 600	ABN 1A	12/63
Bootle	EM	AEM 1	4/60	DEM 11	AEM 1B	1/64
Bournemouth	EL, RU, LJ	AEL 1	5/34	670 CLJ	AEL 1B	4/64
Bradford	AK, KU, KW, KY	AAK 1	5/35	1166 KY	AAK 1B	6/64
Breconshire	EU	AEU 1	10/49	PEU 511	AEU 1C	1/65
Brighton	CD, UF	ACD 1	5/33	812 FCD	ACD 1B	7/64
Bristol	AE, HT, HU, HW, HY	AAE 1	7/33	408 YAE	AAE 1B	9/64
Buckinghamshire	BH, PP, KX	ABH 1	3/33	6200 PP	ABH 1B	4/64
Burnley	CW, HG	ACW 1	9/48	RCW 471	ACW 1B	3/64
Burton-on-Trent	FA	AFA 1	6/50	UFA 718	AFA 1B	5/64
Bury	EN	AEN 1	12/49	VEN 193	AEN 1B	9/64
Bute	SJ	—		SJ 2860	ASJ 1B	1/64
Caernarvonshire	CC, JC	ACC 1	2/49	OJC 362	ACC 1B	8/64
Caithness	SK	ASK 1	8/63	ASK 871	ASK 1B	8/64
Cambridgeshire	CE, ER, VE	ACE 1	2/34	7 EVE	ACE 1B	3/64
Canterbury	FN, JG	AFN 1	11/37	1473 JG	AFN 1B	1/64
Cardiff	BO, UH, KG	ABO 1	1/37	866 FKG	ABO 1B	2/64
Cardiganshire	EJ	AEJ 1	6/49	SEJ 726	AEJ 1B	9/64
Carlisle	HH	AHH 1	3/38	YHH 820	AHH 1B	1/64
Carlow	IC	AIC 1	4/64	YIC 994	87-CW-1	1/87
Carmarthenshire	BX, TH	ABX 1	3/38	820 FBX	ABX 1B	7/64
Cavan	ID	AID 1	7/58	906 IID	87-CN-1	1/87
Cheshire	M, MA, MB, TU, LG	ALG 1	11/32	5742 TU	ALG 1B	1/64

70

Authorities 1903-1974

Authority	One- and two- letter marks in order of issue	First 3-letter mark with date of issue		Last normal mark before year identifiers	First 'year-identifier' mark with date of issue	
Chester	FM	AFM 1	10/35	8417 FM	AFM 1B	6/64
Clackmannanshire	SL	—		SL 9602	ASL 1B	7/64
Clare	IE	AIE 1	3/59	107 XIE	87-CE-1	1/87
Cork (City)	PI, ZF	API 1	12/58	542 FZF	87-C-1	1/87
Cork (County)	IF, ZB, ZK, ZT	AIF 1	12/55	*		
Cornwall	AF, RL, CV	AAF 1	3/34	983 WRL	AAF 1B	9/64
Coventry	DU, HP, RW, WK, VC, KV	ADU 1	7/34	9352 KV	ADU 1B	6/64
Croydon	BY, RK, VB, OY	ABY 1	9/34	999 EOY	ABY 1C	1/65
Cumberland	AO, RM	AAO 1	12/33	826 MRM	AAO 1B	3/64
Darlington	HN	AHN 1	6/34	122 YHN	AHN 1B	9/64
Denbighshire	CA, UN	ACA 1	7/36	530 BCA	ACA 1B	6/64
Derby	CH, RC	ACH 1	4/47	672 FCH	ACH 1B	2/64
Derbyshire	R, NU, RA, RB	ANU 1	1/34	3493 RA	ANU 1B	6/64
Devon	T, TA, TT, UO, DV, OD	ATA 1	6/34	240 TOD	ATA 1B	7/64
Dewsbury	HD	AHD 1	11/53	LHD 750	AHD 1B	9/64
Doncaster	DT	ADT 1	4/38	400 RDT	ADT 1B	5/64
Donegal	IH, ZP	AIH 1	11/61	4853 ZP	87-DL-1	1/87
Dorset	FX, PR, TK, JT	AFX 1	10/38	VTK 500	AFX 1B	3/64
Down	IJ, BZ, JZ, SZ	AIJ 1	5/67	—	—	
Dublin (City)	RI, YI, ZI, ZA, ZC, ZD, ZH, ZJ, ZL, SI, ZG, ZS	† ARI 1	5/54	ZS 8709	87-D-1	1/87
Dublin (County)	IK, Z, ZE, ZO, ZU, ZV					
Dudley	FD	AFD 1	10/35	581 EFD	AFD 1B	7/64
Dumfriesshire	SM	ASM 1	6/33	344 FSM	ASM 1B	7/64
Dunbartonshire	SN	ASN 1	10/46	VSN 555	ASN 1B	8/64
Dundee	TS, YJ	ATS 1	1/48	STS 126	ATS 1B	8/64
Durham	J, PT, UP	APT 1	12/34	751 MUP	APT 1B	2/64
Eastbourne	HC, JK	AHC 1	9/49	MJK 46	AHC 1B	8/64
East Ham	HM, HV	AHM 1	5/38	YHV 355	AHM 1B	5/64
East Lothian	SS	BSS 1	11/55	HSS 439	JSS 1B	3/64
Edinburgh	S, SG, SF, SC, FS, WS	AFS 1	7/36	415 FS	AFS 1B	2/64
Ely, Isle of	EB, JE	AEB 1	8/47	RJE 6	AEB 1B	4/64
Essex	F, HK, NO, PU, TW, VW, VX, EV, OO, WC	AEV 1	3/33	950 YWC	AEV 1A	11/63
Exeter	FJ	AFJ 1	8/34	200 JFJ	AFJ 1B	2/64
Fermanagh	IL	AIL 1	8/66	—	—	
Fife	SP, FG	AFG 1	10/34	7918 FG	AFG 1B	5/64
Flintshire	DM	ADM 1	7/36	88 JDM	ADM 1B	3/64
Galway	IM, ZM	AIM 1	11/59	797 GZM	87-G-1	1/87
Gateshead	CN	ACN 1	4/46	SCN 56	ACN 1B	7/64
Glamorganshire	L, NY, TX, TG	ANY 1	4/35	955 XTX	ANY 1B	5/64
Glasgow	G, US, GA, GB, GD, GE, GG, YS	AGA 1	9/36	344 KGE	AGA 1B	1/64
Gloucester	FH	AFH 1	1/36	286 FFH	AFH 1B	6/64
Gloucestershire	AD, DD, DF, DG	AAD 1	9/34	4510 DG	AAD 1B	1/64
Great Yarmouth	EX	AEX 1	7/56	KEX 712	AEX 1B	3/64
Greenock	VS	AVS 1	12/59	EVS ???	EVS???B	4/64
Grimsby	EE, JV	AEE 1	1/47	YJV 800	AEE 1B	7/64
Halifax	CP, JX	ACP 1	5/47	UCP 24	ACP 1B	6/64
Hampshire	AA, HO, OR, OT, OU, CG	AAA 1	12/34	4 NOU	AAA 1C	1/65

*Issued jointly with Cork City (County Borough Council) from 1985.
†Dublin City (County Borough Council) and County became a joint authority in 1952.

Authorities 1903-1974

Authority	One- and two-letter marks in order of issue	First 3-letter mark with date of issue		Last normal mark before year identifiers	First 'year-identifier' mark with date of issue	
Hastings	DY	ADY 1	2/37	VDY 479	ADY 1B	6/64
Herefordshire	CJ, VJ	ACJ 1	4/37	127 EVJ	ACJ 1B	1/64
Hertfordshire	AR, NK, RO, UR, JH	ANK 1	6/34	?500 WAR	AAR 1B	3/64
Huddersfield	CX, VH	ACX 1	1/37	YVH 900	ACX 1A	8/63
Hull	AT, KH, RH	AAT 1	6/34	909 HKH	AAT 1B	5/64
Huntingdonshire	EW	AEW 1	3/37	749 MEW	AEW 1B	7/64
Invernessshire	ST	AST 1	1/39	YST 219	AST 1C	1/65
Ipswich	DX, PV	ADX 1	1/50	UPV 894	ADX 1B	8/64
Kent	D, KT, KN, KE, KK, KL, KM, KO, KP, KR, KJ	AKE 1	11/32	5700 D	AKE 1B	9/64
Kerry	IN, ZX	AIN 1	1/62	375 CIN	87-KY-1	1/87
Kildare	IO, ZW	AIO 1	4/63	9343 ZW	87-KE-1	1/87
Kilkenny	IP	AIP 1	2/55	235 UIP	87-KK-1	1/87
Kincardineshire	SU	ASU 1	8/61	BSU 686	ASU 1B	6/64
Kinrossshire	SV	—		SV 3722	ASV 1B	1/64
Kirkcudbrightshire	SW	ASW 1	1/55	GSW 494	ASW 1B	5/64
Lanarkshire	V, VA, VD	AVA 1	8/38	44 KVA	AVA 1B	6/64
Lancashire	B, TB, TC, TD, TE, TF, TJ	ATB 1	4/35	9700 TJ	ATB 1A	9/63
Laois	CI	ACI 1	7/60	7342 CI	87-LS-1	1/87
Leeds	U, NW, UM, UA, UB, UG	ANW 1	5/34	250 LUG	ANW 1C	1/65
Leicester	BC, RY, JF	ABC 1	1/36	601 HRY	ABC 1B	3/64
Leicestershire	AY, NR, UT, JU	AAY 1	11/36	573 EUT	AAY 1B	2/64
Leitrim	IT	AIT 1	5/72	KIT 780	87-LM-1	1/87
Limerick (City)	TI	ATI 1	10/59	929 FTI	87-L-1	1/87
Limerick (County)	IU, IV	AIU 1	11/54	OIV 520	87-LK-1	1/87
Lincoln	FE, VL	AFE 1	9/37	XVL 280	AFE 1B	9/64
Lincolnshire (Holland)	DO, JL	ADO 1	10/45	YJL 970	ADO 1B	7/64
Lincolnshire (Kesteven)	CT, TL	ACT 1	1/42	YTL 783	ACT 1B	6/64
Lincolnshire (Lindsey)	BE, FU, FW	ABE 1	8/37	424 HFU	ABE 1B	6/64
Liverpool	K, KB, KC, KA, KD, KF, LV	AKA 1	8/34	541 JKB	AKA 1B	5/64
London	A, LC, LN, LB, LD, LA, LE, LF, LH, LK, LL, LM, LO, LP, LR, LT, LU, LW, LX, LY, XA, XB, XC, XD, XE, XF, XH, XK, XL, XM, XN, XO, XP, XR, XT, XU, XW, XX, XY, YK, YL, YM, YN, YO, YP, YR, YE, YF, YH, YT, YU, UC, YV, YW, YX, XV, UL, GU, UU, UV, UW, GC, GF, GJ, GH, GK, GN, GO, GP, GT, GW, GX, GY, YY, JJ	AGC 1	3/33	??? HYH	AGC 1B	4/64
Londonderry (City)	UI	AUI 1	4/73	—	—	
Londonderry (County)	IW, NZ, YZ	AIW 1	10/73	—	—	
Longford	IX	AIX 1	2/70	PIX 710	87-LD-1	1/87
Louth	IY, ZY	AIY 1	1/64	2507 ZY	87-LH-1	1/87
Man, Isle of	MN	MAN 1	3/35	—	MAN 2A	5/74
Manchester	N, NA, NB, NC, ND, NE, NF, VM, VR, VU, XJ	ANA 1	9/33	5603 XJ	ANA 1B	7/64
Mayo	IZ, IS	AIZ 1	10/54	HIS 990	87-MO-1	1/87
Meath	AI, ZN	AAI 1	2/62	88 ZN	87-MH-1	1/87

Authority	One- and two- letter marks in order of issue	First 3-letter mark with date of issue		Last normal mark before year identifiers	First 'year-identifier' mark with date of issue	
Merionethshire	FF	AFF 1	6/55	HFF 916	AFF 1B	1/64
Merthyr Tydfil	HB	AHB 1	8/58	EHB 383	AHB 1B	4/64
Middlesbrough	DC, XG	ADC 1	4/48	SXG 832	ADC 1B	3/64
Middlesex	H, MX, MC, MD, ME, MF, MH, MK, MM, ML, MP, MT, MY, MU, MG, HX, MV	AMY 1	10/32	NMY ???	AHX 1A	2/63
Midlothian	SY	ASY 1	5/51	NSY 175	ASY 1B	8/64
Monaghan	BI	ABI 1	3/61	6540 BI	87-MN-1	1/87
Monmouthshire	AX, WO	AAX 1	7/35	994 JWO	AAX 1B	3/64
Montgomeryshire	EP	AEP 1	11/47	TEP 654	AEP 1C	1/65
Moray	SO	ASO 1	2/52	MSO 930	ASO 1B	9/64
Motherwell & Wishaw	GM	AGM 1	2/59	FGM 950	AGM 1A	10/63
Nairnshire	AS	—		AS 4097	AAS 1C	1/65
Newcastle upon Tyne	BB, TN, VK	ABB 1	7/33	812 XBB	ABB 1B	1/64
Newport	DW	ADW 1	4/36	5316 DW	ADW 1B	7/64
Norfolk	AH, PW, VF, NG	AAH 1	5/35	35 EPW	AAH 1B	1/64
Northampton	NH, VV	ANH 1	2/47	TVV 757	ANH 1B	7/64
Northamptonshire	BD, RP, NV	ABD 1	10/37	373 GNV	ABD 1B	3/64
Northumberland	X, NL, TY, JR	ANL 1	7/39	YJR 850	AJR 1A	10/63
Norwich	CL, VG	ACL 1	4/37	YVG 130	ACL 1C	1/65
Nottingham	AU, TO, TV	AAU 1	1/34	422 UTO	AAU 1B	2/64
Nottinghamshire	AL, NN, RR, VO	AAL 1	3/33	257 YNN	AAL 1B	9/64
Offaly	IR	AIR 1	5/60	7834 IR	87-OY-1	1/87
Oldham	BU	ABU 1	2/37	167 KBU	ABU 1B	8/64
Orkney	BS	—		BS 7777	ABS 1C	1/65
Oxford	FC, WL, JO	AFC 1	5/34	850 VWL	AFC 1C	1/65
Oxfordshire	BW, UD	ABW 1	10/38·	YUD 800	ABW 1A	11/63
Paisley	XS	AXS 1	7/56	JXS 600	AXS 1B	9/64
Peeblesshire	DS	—		DS 6396	ADS 1C	1/65
Pembrokeshire	DE	ADE 1	7/34	324 YDE	ADE 1C	1/65
Perthshire	ES, GS	AES 1	9/41	VGS 575	AES 1B	2/64
Peterborough, Soke of	FL, EG	AEG 1	11/49	UFL 639	AEG 1B	6/64
Plymouth	CO, DR, JY	ACO 1	2/37	YJY 999	ACO 1A	9/63
Portsmouth	BK, TP, RV	ABK 1	11/36	870 DRV	ABK 1B	3/64
Preston	CK, RN	ACK 1	12/39	VCK 530	ACK 1B	7/64
Radnorshire	FO	AFO 1	8/58	EFO 543	AFO 1B	8/64
Reading	DP, RD	ADP 1	7/37	2113 RD	ADP 1B	6/64
Renfrewshire	HS	AHS 1	6/37	YHS 964	AHS 1B	3/64
Rochdale	DK	ADK 1	4/35	7633 DK	ADK 1B	6/64
Roscommon	DI	ADI 1	1/63	292 BDI	87-RN-1	1/87
Ross & Cromarty	JS	AJS 1	9/52	NJS 333	AJS 1B	3/64
Rotherham	ET	AET 1	10/30	840/ ET	AET 1C	1/65
Roxburghshire	KS	AKS 1	4/47	SKS 12	AKS 1B	6/64
Rutland	FP	AFP 1	8/60	DFP 136	AFP 1B	1/64
St Helens	DJ	ADJ 1	9/47	XDJ 280	ADJ 1B	1/64
Salford	BA, RJ	ABA 1	4/38	YRJ 899	ABA 1A	11/63
Selkirkshire	LS	—		LS 9583	ALS 1B	4/64
Sheffield	W, WA, WB, WF, WJ	AWA 1	4/34	345 JWB	AWA 1B	2/64
Shetland	PS	—		PS 4080	APS 1C	1/65
Shropshire	AW, NT, UX, UJ	AAW 1	6/37	4757 NT	AAW 1B	2/64
Sligo	EI	AEI 1	11/59	835 AEI	87-SO-1	1/87
Smethwick	HA	AHA 1	8/34	?9712 HA	AHA 1B	8/64

Authorities 1903-1974

Authority	One- and two- letter marks in order of issue	First 3-letter mark with date of issue		Last normal mark before year identifiers	First 'year-identifier' mark with date of issue	
Somerset	Y, YA, YB, YC, YD	AYA 1	7/34	56 YYC	AYA 1B	8/64
Southampton	CR, TR, OW	ACR 1	8/36	208 HTR	ACR 1B	7/64
Southend-on-Sea	HJ, JN	AHJ 1	12/37	4938 JN	AHJ 1B	5/64
Southport	FY, WM	AFY 1	2/34	YWM 757	AFY 1B	2/64
South Shields	CU	ACU 1	11/57	NCU 125	ACU 1C	1/65
Staffordshire	E, RE, RF, BF	ARF 1	7/32	600 YBF	ARE 1A	7/63
Stirlingshire	MS, WG	AMS 1	7/43	XWG 918	AMS 1B	2/64
Stockport	DB, JA	ADB 1	1/38	YJA 999	ADB 1A	10/63
Stoke-on-Trent	EH, VT	AEH 1	9/33	8975 EH	AEH 1C	1/65
Suffolk (East)	BJ, RT	ABJ 1	10/33	349 WBJ	ABJ 1B	7/64
Suffolk (West)	CF, GV	ACF 1	4/46	YGV 976	ACF 1B	8/64
Sunderland	BR, GR	ABR 1	6/48	YBR 319	ABR 1B	8/64
Surrey	P, PA, PB, PC, PD, PE, PF, PH, PK, PG, PL, PJ	APA 1	10/32	8000 PE	APA 1B	1/64
Sussex (East)	AP, PM, PN, NJ	AAP 1	10/36	9042 AP	AAP 1B	2/64
Sussex (West)	BP, PX, PO	ABP 1	6/34	670 PBP	ABP 1B	5/64
Sutherland	NS	—		NS 5685	ANS 1B	7/64
Swansea	CY, WN	ACY 1	6/36	950 JCY	ACY 1B	5/64
Tipperary (N. Riding)	FI	AFI 1	1/58	418 JFI	87-TN-1	1/87
Tipperary (S. Riding)	HI, GI	AHI 1	9/54	CGI 871	87-TS-1	1/87
Tynemouth	FT	AFT 1	2/57	KFT 333	AFT 1B	8/64
Tyrone	JI, HZ, VZ	AJI 1	6/71	—	—	
Wakefield	HL	AHL 1	4/43	4151 HL	AHL 1B	8/64
Wallasey	HF	AHF 1	10/46	OHF 835	AHF 1C	1/65
Walsall	DH	ADH 1	6/33	5860 DH	ADH 1B	9/64
Warrington	ED	AED 1	5/36	8790 ED	AED 2B	9/64
Warwickshire	AC, NX, UE, WD	AAC 1	6/35	247 LNX	AAC 1B	5/64
Waterford (City)	WI	AWI 1	1/66	WWI 80	87-W-1	1/87
Waterford (County)	KI	AKI 1	3/61	586 AKI	87-WD-1	1/87
West Bromwich	EA	AEA 1	12/38	97 UEA	AEA 1C	1/65
West Ham	AN, JD	AAN 1	1/39	459 EAN	AAN 1C	1/65
West Hartlepool	EF	AEF 1	7/51	REF 539	AEF 1B	9/64
West Lothian	SX	ASX 1	2/56	KSX 535	ASX 1B	4/64
Westmeath	LI	ALI 1	6/59	869 GLI	87-WH-1	1/87
Westmorland	EC, JM	AEC 1	11/50	MJM 180	AEC 1B	8/64
Wexford	MI, ZR	AMI 1	5/61	8071 ZR	87-WX-1	1/87
Wicklow	NI	ANI 1	5/57	426 TNI	87-WW-1	1/87
Wigan	EK, JP	AEK 1	8/52	LJP 578	AEK 1B	8/64
Wight, Isle of	DL	ADL 1	10/35	522 CDL	ADL 1B	2/64
Wigtownshire	OS	AOS 1	7/55	HOS 692	AOS 1B	9/64
Wiltshire	AM, HR, MR, MW, WV	AAM 1	2/36	277 EMW	AAM 1B	6/64
Wolverhampton	DA, UK, JW	ADA 1	7/36	92 GDA	ADA 1B	5/64
Worcester	FK	AFK 1	3/42	975 YFK	AFK 1B	6/64
Worcestershire	AB, NP, UY, WP	AAB 1	10/35	520 MUY	AAB 1B	1/64
York	DN, VY	ADN 1	8/37	?3000 VY	ADN 1B	8/64
Yorkshire (E. Riding)	BT, WF	ABT 1	3/37	839 CBT	ABT 1B	6/64
Yorkshire (N. Riding)	AJ, PY, VN	AAJ 1	2/37	281 HAJ	AAJ 1B	5/64
Yorkshire (W. Riding)	C, WR, WY, WT, WU, WW, WX, YG	AWR 1	1/35	58 HWR	AWR 1B	3/64

YEAR LETTERS (AGE IDENTIFIERS) FROM JANUARY 1963 TO AUGUST 2001 (Great Britain only)

Suffix letters were used between January 1963 and July 1983. Example: AEF 29T was issued between 1 August 1978 and 31 July 1979.

Prefix letters were used between August 1983 and August 2001. Example: W477 UAG was issued between 1 March 2000 and 31 August 2000.

Suffix	Date	Prefix	Date
A	January - December 1963	A	August 1983 - July 1984
B	January - December 1964	B	August 1984 - July 1985
C	January - December 1965	C	August 1985 - July 1986
D	January - December 1966	D	August 1986 - July 1987
E	January - July 1967	E	August 1987 - July 1988
F	August 1967 - July 1968	F	August 1988 - July 1989
G	August 1968 - July 1969	G	August 1989 - July 1990
H	August 1969 - July 1970	H	August 1990 - July 1991
J	August 1970 - July 1971	J	August 1991 - July 1992
K	August 1971 - July 1972	K	August 1992 - July 1993
L	August 1972 - July 1973	L	August 1993 - July 1994
M	August 1973 - July 1974	M	August 1994 - July 1995
N	August 1974 - July 1975	N	August 1995 - July 1996
P	August 1975 - July 1976	P	August 1996 - July 1997
R	August 1976 - July 1977	R	August 1997 - July 1998
S	August 1977 - July 1978	S	August 1998 - February 1999
T	August 1978 - July 1979	T	March - August 1999
V	August 1979 - July 1980	V	September 1999 - February 2000
W	August 1980 - July 1981	W	March - August 2000
X	August 1981 - July 1982	X	September 2000 - February 2001
Y	August 1982 - July 1983	Y	March - August 2001

Q prefix reserved for vehicles whose date of manufacture is unknown (see page 37).

O used as a prefix in the Isle of Man but is not a year letter (see page 39).

U used as a suffix and prefix in the Isle of Man but is not a year letter (see page 39).

On 1 October 1974, during the N suffix period, the responsibility for issuing registration marks was handed over from Local Taxation Offices (LTOs) to Local Vehicle Licensing Offices (LVLOs) in conjunction with the new computer centre (DVLC) at Swansea. Generally the new LVLOs took over the two-letter marks from the LTOs in their area, e.g. Dumfries office issued the SW series from nearby Kirkcudbrightshire but there were many exceptions (see pages 63-68).

Registration marks issued by LVLOs initially began with the letter G regardless of where the current series had reached. Examples: Barrow LTO which had reached UEO...N was taken over by Barrow LVLO which began at GEO 1N. Aberystwyth LVLO, taking over from Cardiganshire (which had reached UEJ...N) and Merionethshire (which had reached SFF...N) began its registrations at GEJ...N followed by GFF...N.

Age Identifiers - 2001 onwards

REGISTRATION NUMERALS FROM SEPTEMBER 2001 (Great Britain only)

The numerals show the date of issue of the registration mark.

51   September 2001 - February 2002

02	March - August 2002	09	March - August 2009
52	September 2002 - February 2003	59	September 2009 - February 2010
03	March - August 2003	10	March - August 2010
53	September 2003 - February 2004	60	September 2010 - February 2011
04	March - August 2004	11	March - August 2011
54	September 2004 - February 2005	61	September 2011 - February 2012
05	March - August 2005	12	March - August 2012
55	September 2005 - February 2006	62	September 2012 - February 2013
06	March - August 2006	13	March - August 2013
56	September 2006 - February 2007	63	September 2013 - February 2014
07	March - August 2007	14	March - August 2014
57	September 2007 - February 2008	64	September 2014 - February 2015
08	March - August 2008	15	March - August 2015
58	September 2008 - February 2009	65	September 2015 - February 2016

until

48   March - August 2048
98   September 2048 - February 2049

49   March - August 2049
99   September 2049 - February 2050

Examples.

LM52 HHR would indicate that the vehicle was registered between September 2002 and February 2003.

SP04 ABG would indicate that the vehicle was registered between March and August 2004.

REGISTRATION LETTERS FROM SEPTEMBER 2001 (Great Britain only)

The first letter of a new-format registration mark is a Local Memory Tag to show the area of registration.

A	Anglia	**M**	Manchester and Merseyside
B	Birmingham	**N**	North of England
C	Cymru (Wales)	**O**	Oxford
D	Deeside to Shrewsbury	**P**	Preston and Carlisle
E	Essex	**R**	Reading
F	Forest and Fens	**S**	Scotland
G	Garden of England	**V**	Severn Valley
H	Hampshire and Dorset	**W**	West of England
K	Luton and Northampton	**Y**	Yorkshire
L	London		

The first two letters show the DVLA Local Office of registration as listed on the following pages.

Examples.

BC51 AYD would indicate that the vehicle was registered in Birmingham.

SR52 GHP would indicate that the vehicle was registered in Dundee.

The last three letters are individual to each vehicle but otherwise have no special meaning.

SELECT MARKS

Apart from normal marks allocated according to DVLA Local Office area, others are specially issued by DVLA Swansea on application (see pages 32 and 60). The first two letters of these Select marks have no geographical significance but may be the owner's initials or may be chosen for some other reason. Marks with repeated last letters, such as A M51 EK M, are always Select. Some two-letter combinations are issued only as Select marks, e.g. MY51 RZR, UK02 EMT.

REGISTRATION LETTERS FROM SEPTEMBER 2001 (Great Britain only)

AA	Peterborough	BY	SELECT	DU	Shrewsbury	FT	Lincoln
AB	Peterborough			DV	Shrewsbury	FV	Lincoln
AC	Peterborough			DW	Shrewsbury	FW	Lincoln
AD	Peterborough	CA	Cardiff	DX	Shrewsbury	FX	Lincoln
AE	Peterborough	CB	Cardiff	DY	Shrewsbury	FY	Lincoln
AF	Peterborough	CC	Cardiff				
AG	Peterborough	CD	Cardiff				
AH	SELECT	CE	Cardiff	EA	Chelmsford	GA	Maidstone
AJ	Peterborough	CF	Cardiff	EB	Chelmsford	GB	Maidstone
AK	Peterborough	CG	Cardiff	EC	Chelmsford	GC	Maidstone
AL	SELECT	CH	Cardiff	ED	SELECT	GD	Maidstone
AM	Peterborough	CJ	Cardiff	EE	Chelmsford	GE	Maidstone
AN	Peterborough	CK	Cardiff	EF	Chelmsford	GF	Maidstone
		CL	Cardiff	EG	Chelmsford	GG	Maidstone
AO	Norwich	CM	Cardiff	EH	SELECT	GH	Maidstone
AP	Norwich	CN	Cardiff	EJ	Chelmsford	GJ	Maidstone
AR	Norwich	CO	Cardiff	EK	Chelmsford	GK	Maidstone
AS	Norwich			EL	Chelmsford	GL	Maidstone
AT	Norwich	CP	Swansea	EM	Chelmsford	GM	Maidstone
AU	Norwich	CR	Swansea	EN	Chelmsford	GN	Maidstone
		CS	Swansea	EO	Chelmsford	GO	SELECT
AV	Ipswich	CT	Swansea	EP	Chelmsford		
AW	Ipswich	CU	Swansea	ER	Chelmsford	GP	Brighton
AX	Ipswich	CV	Swansea	ES	Chelmsford	GR	Brighton
AY	Ipswich			ET	Chelmsford	GS	Brighton
		CW	Bangor	EU	Chelmsford	GT	Brighton
		CX	Bangor	EV	Chelmsford	GU	Brighton
BA	Birmingham	CY	SELECT	EW	Chelmsford	GV	Brighton
BB	Birmingham			EX	Chelmsford	GW	Brighton
BC	Birmingham			EY	Chelmsford	GX	Brighton
BD	Birmingham	DA	Chester			GY	Brighton
BE	Birmingham	DB	Chester				
BF	Birmingham	DC	Chester	FA	Nottingham		
BG	Birmingham	DD	Chester	FB	Nottingham	HA	Bournemouth
BH	Birmingham	DE	Chester	FC	Nottingham	HB	Bournemouth
BJ	Birmingham	DF	Chester	FD	Nottingham	HC	Bournemouth
BK	Birmingham	DG	Chester	FE	Nottingham	HD	Bournemouth
BL	Birmingham	DH	Chester	FF	Nottingham	HE	Bournemouth
BM	Birmingham	DJ	Chester	FG	Nottingham	HF	Bournemouth
BN	Birmingham	DK	Chester	FH	Nottingham	HG	Bournemouth
BO	Birmingham			FJ	Nottingham	HH	Bournemouth
BP	Birmingham	DL	Shrewsbury	FK	Nottingham	HJ	Bournemouth
BR	Birmingham	DM	Shrewsbury	FL	Nottingham		
BS	Birmingham	DN	Shrewsbury	FM	Nottingham	HK	Portsmouth
BT	Birmingham	DO	Shrewsbury	FN	Nottingham	HL	Portsmouth
BU	Birmingham	DP	Shrewsbury	FP	Nottingham	HM	Portsmouth
BV	Birmingham	DR	SELECT			HN	Portsmouth
BW	Birmingham	DS	Shrewsbury	FR	Lincoln	HO	SELECT
BX	Birmingham	DT	Shrewsbury	FS	Lincoln	HP	Portsmouth

REGISTRATION LETTERS FROM SEPTEMBER 2001 (Great Britain only)

HR	Portsmouth	KM	Northampton	MJ	Manchester	OJ	Oxford
HS	Portsmouth	KN	Northampton	MK	Manchester	OK	*SELECT*
HT	Portsmouth	KO	Northampton	ML	Manchester	OL	Oxford
HU	Portsmouth	KP	Northampton	MM	Manchester	OM	Oxford
HV	Portsmouth	KR	Northampton	MO	*SELECT*	ON	*SELECT*
HW	Portsmouth (for Isle of Wight)	KS	Northampton	MP	Manchester	OO	Oxford
		KT	Northampton	MR	*SELECT*	OP	Oxford
		KU	Northampton	MS	*SELECT*	OR	*SELECT*
HX	Portsmouth	KV	Northampton	MT	Manchester	OS	Oxford
HY	Portsmouth	KW	Northampton	MU	Manchester	OT	Oxford
		KX	Northampton	MV	Manchester	OU	Oxford
		KY	Northampton	MW	Manchester	OV	Oxford
				MX	Manchester	OW	Oxford
JA	*SELECT*			MY	*SELECT*	OX	Oxford
JB	*SELECT*					OY	Oxford
JC	*SELECT*	LA	Wimbledon				
JD	*SELECT*	LB	Wimbledon				
JE	*SELECT*	LC	Wimbledon	NA	Newcastle		
JF	*SELECT*	LD	Wimbledon	NB	Newcastle	PA	Preston
JG	*SELECT*	LE	Wimbledon	NC	Newcastle	PB	Preston
JH	*SELECT*	LF	Wimbledon	ND	Newcastle	PC	Preston
JJ	*SELECT*	LG	Wimbledon	NE	Newcastle	PD	Preston
JK	*SELECT*	LH	Wimbledon	NG	Newcastle	PE	Preston
JL	*SELECT*	LJ	Wimbledon	NH	Newcastle	PF	Preston
JM	*SELECT*			NJ	Newcastle	PG	Preston
JN	*SELECT*	LK	Stanmore	NK	Newcastle	PH	Preston
JO	*SELECT*	LL	Stanmore	NL	Newcastle	PJ	Preston
JP	*SELECT*	LM	Stanmore	NM	Newcastle	PK	Preston
JR	*SELECT*	LN	Stanmore	NN	Newcastle	PL	Preston
JS	*SELECT*	LO	Stanmore	NO	*SELECT*	PM	Preston
JT	*SELECT*	LP	Stanmore			PN	Preston
JU	*SELECT*	LR	Stanmore	NP	Stockton	PO	Preston
JV	*SELECT*	LS	Stanmore	NR	Stockton	PP	Preston
JW	*SELECT*	LT	Stanmore	NS	Stockton	PR	Preston
JX	*SELECT*			NT	Stockton	PS	Preston
JY	*SELECT*	LU	Sidcup	NU	Stockton	PT	Preston
		LV	Sidcup	NV	Stockton		
		LW	Sidcup	NW	Stockton		
KA	Luton	LX	Sidcup	NX	Stockton	PU	Carlisle
KB	Luton	LY	Sidcup	NY	Stockton	PV	Carlisle
KC	Luton					PW	Carlisle
KD	Luton					PX	Carlisle
KE	Luton	MA	Manchester	OA	Oxford	PY	Carlisle
KF	Luton	MB	Manchester	OB	Oxford		
KG	Luton	MC	Manchester	OC	Oxford	RA	Reading
KH	Luton	MD	Manchester	OD	Oxford	RB	Reading
KJ	Luton	ME	Manchester	OE	Oxford	RC	Reading
KK	Luton	MF	Manchester	OF	Oxford	RD	Reading
KL	Luton	MG	Manchester	OG	Oxford	RE	Reading
		MH	Manchester	OH	*SELECT*	RF	Reading

Local Codes - 2001 onwards

REGISTRATION LETTERS FROM SEPTEMBER 2001 (Great Britain only)

RG	Reading	TB	SELECT	VB	Worcester	XA	(Exports) †
RH	Reading	TC	SELECT	VC	Worcester	XB	(Exports) †
RJ	Reading	TD	SELECT	VD	Worcester	XC	(Exports) †
RK	Reading	TE	SELECT	VE	Worcester	XD	(Exports) †
RL	Reading	TF	SELECT	VF	Worcester	XE	(Exports) †
RM	Reading	TG	SELECT	VG	Worcester	XF	(Exports) †
RN	Reading	TH	SELECT	VH	Worcester	XG	SELECT
RO	Reading	TJ	SELECT	VJ	Worcester	XH	SELECT
RP	Reading	TK	SELECT	VK	Worcester	XJ	SELECT
RR	Reading	TL	SELECT	VL	Worcester	XK	SELECT
RS	Reading	TM	SELECT	VM	Worcester	XL	SELECT
RT	Reading	TN	SELECT	VN	Worcester	XM	SELECT
RU	SELECT	TO	SELECT	VO	Worcester	XN	SELECT
RV	Reading	TP	SELECT	VP	Worcester	XO	SELECT
RW	Reading	TR	SELECT	VR	Worcester	XP	SELECT
RX	Reading	TS	SELECT	VS	Worcester	XR	SELECT
RY	Reading	TT	SELECT	VT	Worcester	XS	SELECT
		TU	SELECT	VU	Worcester	XT	SELECT
		TV	SELECT	VV	Worcester	XU	SELECT
SA	Glasgow	TW	SELECT	VW	SELECT	XV	SELECT
SB	Glasgow	TX	SELECT	VX	Worcester	XW	SELECT
SC	Glasgow	TY	SELECT	VY	Worcester	XX	SELECT
SD	Glasgow					XY	SELECT
SE	Glasgow						
SF	Glasgow	UA	SELECT	WA	Exeter	YA	Leeds
SG	Glasgow	UB	SELECT	WB	Exeter	YB	Leeds
SH	Glasgow	UC	SELECT	WC	Exeter	YC	Leeds
SJ	Glasgow	UD	SELECT	WD	Exeter	YD	Leeds
		UE	SELECT	WE	Exeter	YE	Leeds
SK	Edinburgh	UF	SELECT	WF	Exeter	YF	Leeds
SL	Edinburgh	UG	SELECT	WG	Exeter	YG	Leeds
SM	Edinburgh	UH	SELECT	WH	Exeter	YH	Leeds
SN	Edinburgh	UJ	SELECT	WJ	Exeter	YJ	Leeds
SO	Edinburgh	UK	SELECT			YK	Leeds
		UL	SELECT	WK	Truro		
SP	Dundee	UM	SELECT	WL	Truro	YL	Sheffield
SR	Dundee	UN	SELECT			YM	Sheffield
SS	Dundee	UO	SELECT	WM	Bristol	YN	Sheffield
ST	Dundee	UP	SELECT	WN	Bristol	YO	Sheffield
SU	SELECT	UR	SELECT	WO	Bristol	YP	Sheffield
		US	SELECT	WP	Bristol	YR	Sheffield
SV	Aberdeen	UT	SELECT	WR	Bristol	YS	Sheffield
SW	Aberdeen	UU	SELECT	WS	Bristol	YT	Sheffield
		UV	SELECT	WT	Bristol	YU	Sheffield
SX	Inverness	UW	SELECT	WU	Bristol		
SY	Inverness	UX	SELECT	WV	Bristol	YV	Beverley
		UY	SELECT	WW	Bristol	YW	Beverley
				WX	Bristol	YX	Beverley
TA	SELECT	VA	Worcester	WY	Bristol	YY	Beverley

† For VAT-free exports, see page 38

80

MK 5625 (ex Army, 1926)
From 1921 to 1939 military
vehicles carried 'normal' civilian
marks issued by Middlesex
County Council.

RAF 184832 (ex Royal Air
Force 1939-49)
During World War II Royal Air
Force vehicles displayed
distinctive RAF numbers.

57 AR 03 (ex Royal Air Force)
Six-character military marks with
central letters were introduced in
1949.

30 XC 27 (ex Army)
Series XA to XK were issued for
vehicles commissioned in Germany.
This Land Rover was used by the
military police in West Berlin.

44 RB 75 (ex Army)
Owing to the shortage of new
vehicles after World War II
many older vehicles were
rebuilt. They were numbered in
the series RA to RH.

98 RN 49 (Royal Navy) The Royal Navy
use RN for most of their vehicles (except
for fork-lift trucks, etc., registered NE).

14 AY 52 (Royal Air Force)

27 BT 41 (ex Army)
The BT series was used by the
Army for vehicles acquired from
the Royal Navy, Royal Air Force
and other outside sources. This
limousine was formerly Royal
Air Force 43 AM 25.

PB 00 AA (Royal Air Force)
NR 41 AA (Army). A new
computer-generated series, with
central numeral followed by AA, was
introduced in 1993.

36 RN 96 (Royal Navy)

73 KK 33, 67 KF 21
(Royal Air Force 1995, 1990) The K
series (KA to KM) was introduced in
1982 and used for all services.

BS 8295 (DVLA, c.2000). Veterans (pre 1905) needing new registrations are given unused marks from the old Orkney series (from BS 8000 onwards).

DS 8944 (DVLA, c.1990). Unused marks from the old Peeblesshire series (from DS 6574 onwards) were issued for vintage vehicles from 1983 to 1992. This particular mark was later 'cherished' and transferred to a newer car but age-related marks created since 1991 have been non-transferrable.

SV 8840 (DVLA, c.2001). When the DS series was exhausted in 1992, unused marks from the old Kinrossshire series (from SV 4001 onwards) were issued for vintage vehicles.

EDS 221A (Glasgow) Formerly London Transport bus registered 10 CLT in 1962. Many numbers with an A suffix are replacements.

VFF 619 (Lincoln, 1995)
FSL 140 (Leeds, 1999)
AAS 647 (Beverley, 2001)
WYJ 328 (Middlesbrough, 1993)

Age-related marks from old unused Scottish or Welsh series are issued for classic vehicles which need new registrations. These vehicles may have been previously unregistered, or ex-military, or imported, or may have lost their original numbers through cherished transfers.

168 Q02 Temporary import 2002

Q57 WDT (Sheffield) Q prefix marks, introduced in 1983, are used for vehicles whose precise age of manufacture is unknown, such as some imports, kit cars and vehicles made up from parts.

Y531 EXP VAT-free export May 2001

QNI 1085 (Northern Ireland)
Q-61-MAN (Isle of Man)
The Northern Ireland and Isle of Man versions of Q prefix marks.

145 AT (Hull/Beverley)
United Kingdom

157-MO-02 (Co Mayo, 2002)
Republic of Ireland

MNA 436 (Isle of Man)

J 144 (Jersey)

T 124 (Guernsey). General trade
plate.
Z 70 (Guernsey). Limited (delivery)
trade plate.

H270HP/99 (Russia) Moscow

D 1916 (Andorra)

B 69 FDR (Romania) Bucharest

FN-AY 368 (Germany) Friedrichshafen

DEV-531 (Belgium)

SR 81666 (Norway) Bergen

EZX 945 (Cyprus) With European Union panel in anticipation of membership.

EQUIPMENT REGISTRATION MARKS (1949-93)

Letters in this list refer to the middle two characters of the two digits, two letters, two digits arrangement, e.g. 06 **SP** 15.

Army equipment categories: Army A = armoured vehicles, B = general transport, C = engineer vehicles, P = mechanical handling equipment (e.g. forklift trucks, platforms, etc.).

AA	R.A.F.(1950-83)	Ambulances, Land Rovers
AB	R.A.F.(1950-83)	Cars
AC	R.A.F.(1950-83)	Coaches and cranes
AD	R.A.F.(1950-83)	Refuellers, fuel transporters and water tankers
AE	R.A.F.(1950-83)	Cargo trucks
AF	R.A.F.(1950-83)	Cargo trucks and cars
AG	R.A.F.(1950-83)	Fire, water, domestic and crash vehicles
AH	R.A.F.(1950-83)	Motor Transport breakdown vehicles
AJ	R.A.F.(1950-83)	Cargo trucks and fire tenders
AK	R.A.F.(1950-83)	Sweepers, snow clearance, refuse vehicles and troop carriers
AL	R.A.F.(1950-83)	Tippers and dumper trucks
AM	R.A.F.(1950-83)	Cars, Land Rovers and minibuses
AN	R.A.F.(1950-83)	Tractors
AO	R.A.F.(1980-3)	Weapons handling equipment for Tornado aircraft
AP	R.A.F.(1950-83)	Stacking and forklift vehicles
AQ	R.A.F.(1950-83)	Snowploughs, snowblowers and de-icing trailers
AR-AS	R.A.F.(1950-83)	Vans and light pick-up trucks
AT	R.A.F.(1950-83)	Combat reconnaisance equipment
AU	R.A.F.(1950-83)	Trailers
AV	R.A.F.(1950-83)	Radio vehicles
AW	R.A.F.(1950-83)	Trailers
AX	R.A.F.(1950-83)	Trailers and motor cycles
AY	R.A.F.	Specialist vehicles and equipment 1982 onwards
AZ	DoE	Department of the Environment vehicles used at airfields
BA-BB	Army A	1949-57
BC-BH,BJ-BN	Army B	1949-54
BP,BR,BS	Army B	1955-7
BT	Army	Miscellaneous, including acquisitions from other armed services
BX	Army	USA vehicles received under Military Assistance Programme

BY	Army C	1949-57
CA	Army A	1957-8
CB	Army	Truck mounted equipment
CC	Army A	1958-9
CE,CL	Army B	1957-9
CP	Army	Construction plant (Royal Engineers)
CV	Army	Captured vehicles in Falklands War 1982
CW,CY	Army C	1957-9
DA,DC,DD	Army A	1959-62
DE,DL,DM	Army B	1959-62
DV	Army	Royal Engineers equipment transferred from RAF
DW-DZ	Army C	1959-62
EA-EE	Army A	1962-7
EK-EN,EP	Army B	1962-5
ER-ET	Army B	1965-7
EU-EW, EY-EZ	Army C	1962-7
FA-FF	Army A	1967-73
FG-FH,FJ-FM	Army B	1967-73
FU-FZ	Army C	1967-73
GA	Army	Special Project Ghana vehicles
GB	Army B	1973-4
GC	Army A	1973-4
GD	Army C	1973-4
GE	Army A	1974-5
GF	Army B	1974-5
GG	Army C	1974-5
GH	Army A	1975-6
GJ	Army B	1975-6
GK	Army C	1975-6
GL	Army P	1975-6
GM	Army A	1976-7
GN	Army B	1976-7
GP	Army C	1976-7
GR	Army P	1976-7
GS	Army A	1977-8
GT	Army B	1977-8
GU	Army C	1977-8
GV	Army P	1977-8
GX	Army B	1977-8
HA-HB,HD-HE	Army A	1978-82
HF-HH,HJ	Army B	1978-82
HP	Army P	1978-83

HV-HZ	Army C	1978-83
KA-KM	All Services	1982-1994 Non-specialist equipment
LV	All Services	Leased vehicles
MH	Army	Mechanical handling equipment (fork lift trucks etc.) 1982 onwards
MS	MoS	Ministry of Supply sales to foreign countries and other outside customers
MW	MoW	Ministry of Works vehicles
NA	NAAFI	NAAFI vehicles in Singapore
NC	All Services	Non-census vehicles (non-contract purchases made by individual units, etc.)
NE	Royal Navy	Mechanical handling equipment (fork lift trucks, etc)
NK	Army	Miscellaneous sales (trailers)
PB	DoE	Department of the Environment vehicles for maintenance of British buildings abroad
RA-RH	Army B	Rebuilt pre-1949 vehicles
RN	Royal Navy	1950 onwards
SP	Army	Special Project research vehicles
TC	Army	Transportable cabins
TF	Army	Fire pump trailers
TG	Army	Mobile guns
TM	Army	Trailer-mounted equipment
TP	All services	Trade (temporary) plates
WA-WB	All services	Research and development equipment
WH	Army	Formerly used by Royal Signals White Helmets Motorcycle Display Team
WL	Army	Far East Land Forces welfare vehicles
WP	DoE	Department of the Environment overseas use
XA-XF	All services	Vehicles commissioned in Germany
XG	All services	Vehicles commissioned in Germany, including Commonwealth War Graves Commission
XH,XJ-XK	All services	Vehicles commissioned in Germany
YA-YH,YJ-YN	Army B	Renumbered pre-1949 vehicles
YP,YR-YZ	Army B	Renumbered pre-1949 vehicles
ZA-ZC	Army B	Renumbered pre-1949 vehicles
ZE	Army P	Mechanical handling equipment (fork lift trucks, etc.) 1949-73
ZF-ZG	Army P	Mechanical handling equipment 1973-5
ZR-ZW	Army A	Renumbered pre-1949 vehicles
ZX-ZY	Army C	Renumbered pre-1949 vehicles (excavators, tractors and mobile cranes)
ZZ	Army B	Canadian vehicles operated in UK

Local Offices

For addresses of DVLA and DVLNI headquarters, see page 109.

Office Codes (see page 104)

301	Aberdeen
304	Dundee
305	Edinburgh
306	Glasgow
307	Inverness
321	Stockton
322	Newcastle
326	Carlisle
329	Manchester
330	Preston
335	Beverley
336	Leeds
337	Sheffield
342	Lincoln
343	Nottingham
346	Ipswich
347	Norwich
348	Peterborough
352	Stanmore
353	Wimbledon
354	Sidcup
357	Brighton

Office Codes (see page 104)

359	Chelmsford
362	Luton
363	Maidstone
365	Northampton
366	Oxford
367	Portsmouth
368	Reading
371	Bournemouth
372	Bristol
373	Exeter
379	Truro
381	Birmingham
385	Worcester
391	Bangor
392	Cardiff
393	Chester
396	Shrewsbury
397	Swansea

92

DVLA LOCAL OFFICES

Greyfriars House, Gallowgate	ABERDEEN	AB10 1WG	0870 240 6279
Penrhos Road, Penrhosgarnedd	BANGOR	LL57 2JF	01248 351822
Crosskill House, Mill Lane	BEVERLEY	HU17 9JB	0870 240 1316
2nd Floor, Edward House, Edward Street	BIRMINGHAM	B1 2RF	0870 240 3518
Tregonwell Court, 118 Commercial Road	BOURNEMOUTH	BH2 5LN	0870 240 4731
4th Floor, Mocatta House, Trafalgar Place,	BRIGHTON	BN1 4UE	0870 240 4732
Northleigh House, Lime Kiln Close, Stoke Gifford	BRISTOL	BS34 8SR	0870 240 1317
Archway House, 77 Ty Glas Avenue, Llanishen	CARDIFF	CF14 5DX	029 20753355
Ground Floor, 3 Merchants Drive, Parkhouse	CARLISLE	CA3 0JW	0870 240 0692
2nd Floor, Parkway House, 49 Baddow Road	CHELMSFORD	CM2 0XJ	0870 241 2147
Norroy House, Nuns Road	CHESTER	CH1 2ND	0870 240 1318
Caledonian House, Greenmarket	DUNDEE	DD1 4QP	0870 240 6280
Department of Transport, Saughton House, Broomhouse Drive	EDINBURGH	EH11 3XE	0870 240 6281
Hanover House, Manaton Close, Matford Business Park, Marsh Barton	EXETER	EX2 8EF	0870 240 4734
46 West Campbell Street	GLASGOW	G2 6TT	0870 240 6282
Longman House, 28 Longman Road	INVERNESS	IV1 1SF	0870 240 6283
Podium Level, St Clare House, Greyfriars	IPSWICH	IP1 1UT	0870 240 8231
1st Floor, 42 Eastgate	LEEDS	LS2 7DQ	0870 240 3514
Firth Court, Firth Road	LINCOLN	LN5 7WD	0870 240 0671
2 Dunstable Road	LUTON	LU1 1EB	0870 240 3515
Coronet House, 11 Queen Anne Road	MAIDSTONE	ME14 1XB	0870 240 3517
Trafford House, Chester Road	MANCHESTER	M32 0SL	0870 241 2146
Eagle Star House, Regent Farm Road	NEWCASTLE UPON TYNE	NE3 3QF	0870 240 0669
Wootton Hall Park	NORTHAMPTON	NN4 0GA	0870 240 8228
11 Prince of Wales Road	NORWICH	NR1 1UP	0870 240 8232
Block 6, Government Buildings, Chalfont Drive	NOTTINGHAM	NG8 3RA	0870 241 1876
Ground Floor, 3 Cambridge Terrace	OXFORD	OX1 1RW	0870 240 8230
88 Lincoln Road	PETERBOROUGH	PE1 2ST	0870 240 8229
5th Floor, Baltic House, Kingston Crescent	PORTSMOUTH	PO2 8AH	0870 240 4730
Fulwood Park, Caxton Road, Fulwood	PRESTON	PR2 9NZ	0870 240 0691
77-81 Basingstoke Road	READING	RG2 0ER	0870 241 5161
Cedar House, Hallamshire Court, 63 Napier Street	SHEFFIELD	S11 8HA	0870 240 1315
Whitehall, Monkmoor Road	SHREWSBURY	SY2 5DR	0870 240 1223
12/18 Station Road	SIDCUP	DA15 7EQ	0870 240 3516
Government Building, Canon Park, Honeypot Lane	STANMORE	HA7 1BD	0870 241 1269
St Marks House, St Marks Court, Thornaby	STOCKTON - ON - TEES	TS17 6QR	0870 240 0695
Heol Pentre Felen	SWANSEA	SA6 7HG	01792 783900
Pydar House, Pydar Street	TRURO	TR1 2TG	0870 240 6278
Ground Floor, Connect House, 133-137 Alexandra Road	WIMBLEDON, LONDON	SW19 7JY	0870 600 6767
Clerkenleap Barn, Broomhall	WORCESTER	WR5 3HR	0870 240 1319

DVLNI LOCAL VEHICLE LICENSING OFFICES

Dobbin Centre, Dobbin Lane	ARMAGH	BT61 7QP	028 3752 7305
County Hall, Galgorm Road	BALLYMENA	BT42 1QE	028 2565 3333
Royston House, Upper Queen Street	BELFAST	BT1 6FA	028 9054 2042
County Hall, Castlerock Road	COLERAINE	BT51 3TA	028 7034 1417
Rathkeltair House, Market Street	DOWNPATRICK	BT30 6AT	028 4461 3211
County Buildings, East Bridge Street	ENNISKILLEN	BT74 7BN	028 6634 6555
Orchard House, 40 Foyle Street	LONDONDERRY	BT48 6AT	028 7131 9900
Boaz House, 15 Scarffe's Entry	OMAGH	BT78 1JE	028 8225 4700

CHANNEL ISLANDS AND ISLE OF MAN

States Office, Queen Elizabeth II Street,	ALDERNEY	GY9 3AA	01481 822811
Vehicle Registration and Licensing Department, Bulwer Avenue, St Sampsons,	GUERNSEY	GY1 3HY	01481 242212
Driver and Vehicle Standards Department, La Collette, St Helier,	JERSEY	JE1 3UE	01534 833200
Vehicle Licensing Department, Central Government Offices, Buck's Road,	DOUGLAS, Isle of Man	IM1 3PX	01624 685600

Republic of Ireland

REGISTRATION MARKS FROM 1 JANUARY 1987

Current Irish registration numbers consist of the last two digits of the year of registration, followed by one or two letters showing the place of registration, followed by a numeral of up to six digits. Hyphens or dots are normally placed between the three sections. The name of the issuing county or city is usually printed in Irish Gaelic in small letters over the number, e.g. **CEATHARLACH** for Carlow.

Numberplates for new cars since 1 January 1987 have black letters and numbers on a reflective white background (both front and rear).

Examples: 99-WH-139 means the vehicle was registered in Westmeath in 1999.
01-D-70668 means the vehicle was registered in Dublin in 2001.

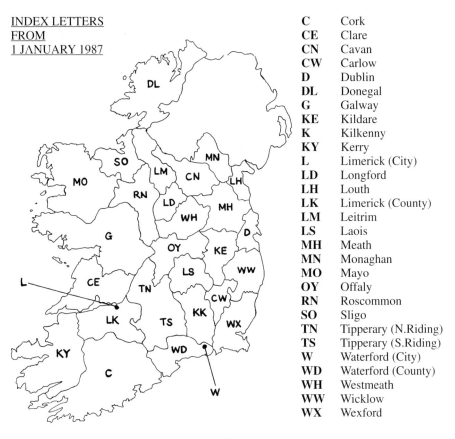

INDEX LETTERS FROM 1 JANUARY 1987		
C	Cork
CE	Clare
CN	Cavan
CW	Carlow
D	Dublin
DL	Donegal
G	Galway
KE	Kildare
K	Kilkenny
KY	Kerry
L	Limerick (City)
LD	Longford
LH	Louth
LK	Limerick (County)
LM	Leitrim
LS	Laois
MH	Meath
MN	Monaghan
MO	Mayo
OY	Offaly
RN	Roscommon
SO	Sligo
TN	Tipperary (N.Riding)
TS	Tipperary (S.Riding)
W	Waterford (City)
WD	Waterford (County)
WH	Westmeath
WW	Wicklow
WX	Wexford

Republic of Ireland

ZV NUMBERS (see page 35)   (C=City, N=North Riding, S=South Riding)

101-300	Carlow	4601-4800	Tipperary N	47701-50200	Longford
301-500	Cavan	4801-5000	Tipperary S	50201-52700	Louth
501-700	Clare	5001-5200	Waterford	52701-55200	Limerick
701-1200	Cork	5201-5400	Westmeath	55201-57700	Leitrim
1201-1400	Donegal	5401-5600	Wexford	57701-60200	Laois
1401-1700	Galway	5601-5800	Wicklow	60201-63200	Meath
1701-2000	Kerry	5801-6800	Dublin	63201-65700	Monaghan
2001-2200	Kildare	6801-7000	Limerick C	65701-68200	Mayo
2201-2400	Kilkenny	7001-7200	Waterford C	68201-70700	Offaly
2401-2600	Laois	7201-17200	Dublin	70701-73200	Roscommon
2601-2800	Leitrim	17201-19700	Clare	73201-75700	Sligo
2801-3000	Limerick	19701-22200	Cavan	75701-78200	Tipperary N
3001-3200	Longford	22201-24700	Carlow	78201-80700	Tipperary S
3201-3400	Louth	24701-30700	Cork	80701-83200	Waterford C
3401-3600	Mayo	30701-33700	Donegal	83201-85700	Waterford
3601-3800	Meath	33701-36700	Galway	85701-88200	Westmeath
3801-4000	Monaghan	36701-39700	Kildare	88201-91200	Wicklow
4001-4200	Offaly	39701-42200	Kilkenny	91201-94200	Wexford
4201-4400	Roscommon	42201-45200	Kerry		
4401-4600	Sligo	45201-47700	Limerick C		

TRAILER NUMBERS

Since 1982 trailers weighing more than 1524 Kg (unladen) have been required to display the registration mark of the towing vehicle and a trailer number consisting of two letters (denoting the county or city of origin) followed by up to four digits. Trailer plates are either white with black characters or reflective red with black characters.

The first letter of a trailer number signifies the province of origin (A = Leinster, B = Munster, C = Connacht, D = Part of Ulster)

AB	Carlow	AO	Meath	BK	Tipperary SR
AC	Dublin	AP	Offaly	BL	Waterford County
AD	Dublin	AR	Westmeath	BM	Waterford City
AE	Dublin	AS	Wexford	CD	Galway
AF	Dublin	AT	Wicklow	CE	Leitrim
AG	Dublin	BC	Clare	CF	Mayo
AH	Dublin	BD	Cork County	CG	Roscommon
AJ	Kildare	BE	Cork City	CH	Sligo
AK	Kilkenny	BF	Kerry	DE	Cavan
AL	Laois	BG	Limerick County	DF	Donegal
AM	Longford	BH	Limerick City	DG	Monaghan
AN	Louth	BJ	Tipperary NR		

Republic of Ireland

VEHICLE REGISTRATION AND MOTOR TAXATION OFFICES

Each county in the Republic of Ireland has separate Vehicle Registration and Motor Taxation offices.

Vehicle Registration Offices are responsible for:-
Registration of new and imported vehicles;
Allocation of registration marks;
Collection of Vehicle Registration Tax.

Motor Taxation Offices are responsible for:-
Taxation of vehicles (tax discs);
Changes of vehicle ownership (for vehicles registered before 1993);*
Car testing and issuing of certificates of roadworthiness.

Some Motor Taxation Offices also hold surviving records of old vehicle registrations. Details can be found in 'Locations of Surviving Local Taxation Office Records' published by the Kithead Trust (see page 106).

Written enquiries should be sent to **Vehicle Registration Office** or **Motor Taxation Office**, followed by the address given for each county or city (followed by **Irish Republic** if posted outside the Republic).

Applications for **reserved numbers** (see page 62) should be sent to Registration Section, Central Vehicle Office, ROSSLARE HARBOUR, Co Wexford (telephone 053 61247).

If telephoning from the U.K., the 0 at the beginning of the number should be replaced by 00353, e.g. Offaly Motor Taxation Office 00353 506 21419.

VEHICLE REGISTRATION OFFICES

CARLOW	6-8 Staplestown Road, CARLOW	0503 31475
CAVAN	New Court Centre, Church Street, CAVAN	049 4362072
CLARE	Government Buildings, Kilrush Road, ENNIS, Co Clare	065 8641200
CORK	Custom House, Sullivan's Quay, CORK	021 4968783
DONEGAL	Bridgend, LIFFORD, Co Donegal	077 68800
	Road Station, LIFFORD, Co Donegal	074 72700
DUBLIN	St John's House, High Street, Tallaght, DUBLIN 24	01 4149777
	Unit 11, Furry Park Industrial Estate, Santry, DUBLIN 9	01 8579800
	111 Lower George's Street, DUN LAOGHAIRE,	
	Co Dublin	01 2020851
GALWAY	Custom House, Flood Street, GALWAY	091 567191
KERRY	Government Buildings, TRALEE, Co Kerry	066 7121480
KILDARE	St David's House, North Main Street, NAAS, Co Kildare	045 880508
KILKENNY	Government Buildings, Hebron Road, KILKENNY	056 52355
LAOIS	Government Buildings, Old Abbeyleix Road,	
	PORTLAOISE, Co Laois	0502 60581

*Changes of ownership for vehicles registered from 1993 onwards are carried out by the Vehicle Registration Centre, SHANNON, Co Clare.

LEITRIM	Government Buildings, By-Pass Road,	
	CARRICK-ON-SHANNON, Co Leitrim	078 21444
LIMERICK	Sarsfield House, Francis Street, LIMERICK	061 415366
LONGFORD	Richmond Street, LONGFORD	043 47018
LOUTH	St Patrick's Hall, DUNDALK, Co Louth	042 9334191
	Carrickcarnan, DUNDALK, Co Louth	042 9371386
MAYO	Government Offices, Michael Davitt House,	
	CASTLEBAR, Co Mayo	094 21131
MEATH	Commons Road, NAVAN, Co Meath	046 75400
MONAGHAN	Coolshannagh, MONAGHAN	047 82800
OFFALY	Government Buildings, TULLAMORE, Co Offaly	0506 25808
ROSCOMMON	Castle Street, ROSCOMMON	0903 25784
SLIGO	Government Buildings, Unit 2, The Quay, SLIGO	071 69180
TIPPERARY (North)	Government Buildings, NENAGH, Co Tipperary	067 33533
TIPPERARY (South)	Harbour House, The Quay, CLONMEL, Co Tipperary	052 26655
WATERFORD	New Civic Office, DUNGARVAN, Co Waterford	058 48150
	Government Buildings, The Glen, WATERFORD	051 877011
WESTMEATH	Spoutwell Lane, MULLINGAR, Co Westmeath	044 42222
WEXFORD	Anne Street, WEXFORD	053 46714
WICKLOW	Government Offices, The Murrough, WICKLOW	0404 68981

MOTOR TAXATION OFFICES

CARLOW	Athy Road, CARLOW	0503 70342
CAVAN	Courthouse, CAVAN	049 4373590
CLARE	Francis Street, ENNIS, Co Clare	065 6844661
CORK	Farranlea Road, CORK	021 4544566
DONEGAL	County House, LIFFORD, Co Donegal	074 72266
DUBLIN	River House, Chancery Street, DUBLIN 7	01 8899222
GALWAY	County Hall, Prospect Hill, GALWAY	091 509304
KERRY	Rathass, TRALEE, Co Kerry	066 7122300
KILDARE	Friary Road, NAAS, Co Kildare	045 897400
KILKENNY	County Hall, John Street, KILKENNY	056 52699
LAOIS	County Hall, PORTLAOISE, Co Laois	0502 22044
LEITRIM	Park Lane House, CARRICK-ON-SHANNON,	
	Co Leitrim	078 20005
LIMERICK (City)	City Hall, Merchants Quay, LIMERICK	061 417122
LIMERICK (County)	Lower Mallow Street, LIMERICK	061 316444
LONGFORD	Great Water Street, LONGFORD	043 46231
LOUTH	Millennium Centre, Alphonsus Road, DUNDALK,	
	Co Louth	042 9335457
MAYO	Glenpark, The Mall, CASTLEBAR, Co Mayo	094 24444
MEATH	County Hall, NAVAN, Co Meath	046 22416
MONAGHAN	Market Street, MONAGHAN	047 81175
OFFALY	O'Connor Square, TULLAMORE, Co Offaly	0506 21419
ROSCOMMON	Abbey Street, ROSCOMMON	0903 37230
SLIGO	Cleveragh Development Centre, SLIGO	071 62221
TIPPERARY (North)	Kickham Street, NENAGH, Co Tipperary	067 44701
TIPPERARY (South)	Emmet Street, CLONMEL, Co Tipperary	052 25399
WATERFORD (City)	The Deanery, Cathedral Square, WATERFORD	051 309951
WATERFORD (County)	Civic Offices, Davitts Quay, DUNGARVAN,	
	Co Waterford	058 22087
WESTMEATH	Church Avenue, MULLINGAR, Co Westmeath	044 32181
WEXFORD	County Hall, Spawell Road, WEXFORD	053 42211
WICKLOW	County Buildings, Whitegates, WICKLOW	0404 20118

97

Civic and Official Cars

Many official cars of city, town and county councils in the U.K. carry cherished marks. Some of these are early registrations originally issued by the councils themselves or their predecessors, such as FC 1 (Oxford's very first registration in December 1903) or 1 CFJ (issued by Exeter council in 1960). Others have been chosen because they have significant 'initials', such as NBC 1W for Nuneaton and Bedworth Council. A few have been specially 'created', such as 1 EA for West Bromwich (now Sandwell) and several 'zero' marks issued mainly for Scottish councils.

C=Chairman, CE=Chief Executive, Con=Convenor, DM=Deputy Mayor, L=Leader, LL=Lord Lieutenant, LM=Lord Mayor, LP=Lord Provost, M=Mayor, P= Provost, S=Sheriff, VC=Vice Chairman.

Aberdeen (LP)	RG 0	Croydon (M)	1 VB
Argyll & Bute (CE,Con,L)	N100 ABC	Derbyshire (C)	R1 DCC
Barnsley (M)	THE 1	Devon (C)	J1 DCC
Belfast (LM)	1 WZ	Doncaster (M)	KDT 1D
Bexley (M)	H7 BEX	Dudley (M)	1 FD
Birmingham (LM)	LOM 1	Dundee (LP)	TS 1
Blackburn (M)	CB 1,	Ealing (M)	RME 1L
	ACB 1	East Renfrewshire (P)	HS 0
Blackpool (M,C,CE)	FV 1	Edinburgh (LP)	S 0, S 10,
Bolton (M)	WH 1		SS 10
Bournemouth (M)	EL 1	Essex (C,CE,L,LL)	F1, 1F
Bradford (LM)	PKW 1M	Exeter (M,DM)	1 CFJ
Brighton & Hove (M,DM)	CD 1,	Fareham (M)	T1 FBC
	H2 OVE	Fermanagh (C)	CIL 606
Bristol (LM)	AE 1	Fylde (M)	930 FBM †
Bromley (M)	LBB 1L	Gateshead (M)	GCN 1
Burnley (M)	HG 1	Glasgow (LP)	G 0, V 0
Bury (M)	T6 BUR	Gosport (M)	1 NCG
Cardiff (LM)	KG 1	Guildford (M)	585 XHN
Cheshire (C)	TTU 1	Hastings (M)	DY 1
Chesterfield (M)	GVU 1V	High Peak (M,L)	H1 PBK
Clackmannanshire (P)	SL 1 *	Hull (LM)	KH 1, 1 KH
Crewe & Nantwich (M)	CMB 1	Inverclyde (P)	VS 0

* On loan from the Earl of Mar
† On loan from Box Bros Ltd

Kent (C)	1 XKT	Portsmouth (LM)	BK 1
Kingston-upon-Thames(M)	RBK 1	Preston (M)	CCK 1
Kirklees (M)	MVH 1	Rochdale (M)	DK 1
Lancaster (M)	L 50	Rotherham (M)	ET 1
Leeds (LM)	U 1	Rugby (M)	MWD 1
Leicester (LM)	ABC 1,	St Helens (M)	CDJ 1
	1 ABC	Salford (M)	RJ 1
Lichfield (C)	X100 LDC	Sandwell (M,L,CE)	1 HA, 1 EA
Lincoln (M)	JFE 1	Scarborough (M)	XVN 1K
London (LM)	LM 0	Sefton (M,DM)	FFY 1,
Macclesfield (M)	MAC 631V		XWM 1M
Maidstone (M)	1 MKP	Shrewsbury & Atcham(M)	J8 SAB
Manchester (LM)	N 10	Slough (M)	MPP 1
Mansfield (C)	GRR 1	Solihull (M)	SOL 1
Midlothian (P)	SY 0	South Lanarkshire (P,L)	R100 SLC
Newcastle upon Tyne(LM)	OBB 1	Southampton (M)	TR 1
Newham (M)	N1 LBN	Southend-on-Sea (M)	HJ 1
Newport (Wales) (M)	NDW 1	Stockport (M)	JJA 1
Newtownabbey (M)	B1 NBC	Stockton-on-Tees (M)	SDC 1M
North East Lincolnshire(M)	M100 NEL	Stoke-on-Trent (LM)	1 VT
North Lanarkshire (P)	AXB 1B	Sunderland (M)	OGR 1
North Lincolnshire (M)	L1 NLC	Walsall (M)	DH 1
North Somerset (C)	NSC 6P	Warrington (M)	ED 1
Northampton (M)	NH 1	Westminster (LM,M)	WE 1
Nottingham (LM,S)	NTV 1,	Wigan (M)	AEK 1,
	NTV 2		NEK 1W
Nuneaton & Bedworth	NBC 1W	Windsor & Maidenhead(M)	K11 RWM
(M,DM,L)		Woking (M)	H1 WBC
Oldham (M)	ABU 1	Wolverhampton (M)	JDA 1
Oxford (LM)	FC 1	Wrexham (M)	H1 WMB
Perth & Kinross (P)	ES 1	Wyre (M)	WBC 74
Peterborough (M)	EG 1	York (LM)	DN 1
Plymouth (LM)	HJY 1	Yorkshire, East Riding	1 BBB,
Poole (M)	APR 1	(C,VC,LL)	GWF 1

Diplomatic Cars

Special registration marks are issued by DVLA for use on the 'flag cars' of the heads of diplomatic missions (embassies, high commissions, consulates, etc.) in London. These marks, often incorporating the single number 1, have letters usually pertaining to the names of the countries whose missions they represent. There are about 140 altogether, some of which are 'cherished' from normal series, such as FGN 1, and others which are 'created' to suit the country and would not normally be issued, such as QUE 1. The first of these special marks, NZ 1, was reserved for the New Zealand High Commission in 1949.

As circumstances change, so do diplomatic marks. New countries, and therefore new diplomatic missions, are created from time to time; other countries alter their names or cease to exist. Sometimes the special number is exchanged for a new one or abandoned altogether, e.g. 1 ROU formerly on the Uruguayan ambassador's car.

The list on the opposite page shows only those currently-used marks whose inclusion in this book has been approved by the missions concerned. It is, however, often easy to guess the identities from the registration letters. Also, cars with this type of registration mark display distinctive five-yearly tax discs which make them readily recognisable.

Apart from the 'cherished' marks reserved for heads of missions, a separate series of special marks is issued for use by other diplomatic or consular staff. These marks, introduced in 1979, consist of a three-digit number code followed by the letter D for diplomatic staff or X for consular or non-diplomatic staff, followed by three further digits, e.g. 231 D 128. The left-hand three digits normally identify the mission, e.g. 174 for Iceland, but numbers 350 to 800 are 'anonymous' for security reasons. Numbers from 900 onwards identify staff of international organisations, e.g. 918 for the Western European Union. On the actual numberplates, the numerals on either side of the middle letter are usually in a distinctive, thinner style. Lists of the three-digit identifiers can be found in 'Registration Plates of the World' and 'The Interpol Guide to Vehicle Registration Plates' (see page 106).

Diplomatic marks of both the kinds mentioned above are issued through DVLA Local Office in Wimbledon but it should be stressed that no official information about these registrations is publicly available.

In addition to their special registration marks, diplomatic cars often carry the letters CD (Corps Diplomatique) on an oval 'international' plate or sticker which is issued by the country of origin and displayed either on the numberplate(s) or on the back of the vehicle.

A = Ambassador, AG = Agent General, DHC = Deputy High Commissioner, HC = High Commissioner.

Algeria(A)	ALG 1A	Kyrgyzstan (A)	1 KYR
Angola (A)	ANG 2	Lebanon (A)	1 RL
Austria (A)	1 OES	Macedonia (A)	1 MAK
Bangladesh (HC)	BDH 1	Malawi (HC)	1 MLW
Belgium (A)	1 BE	Malaysia (HC)	1 M
Belize (HC)	BEL 12E	Maldives (HC)	7 MLD
Bolivia (A)	BOL 1	Malta (HC)	1 MLT
Brazil (A)	BRZ 1	Myanmar (A)	1 MYN
Brunei (HC)	1 NBD	Namibia (HC)	1 NAM
Bulgaria (A)	BG 1	Nepal (A)	NEP 1
Canada (HC,DHC)	CAN 1,	Netherlands (A)	NL 1
	CDA 2	New Zealand (HC)	NZ 1
Chile (A)	CHI 1	Nigeria (HC)	FGN 1
Colombia (A)	COL 1	Norway (A)	1 NWY
Congo (Dem.Republic)(A)	CDR 1	Panama (A)	PAN 1
Côte d'Ivoire (A)	1 RCI	Papua New Guinea (HC)	1 PNG
Croatia (A)	1 HRV	Paraguay (A)	1 PY
Czech Republic (A)	1 CZE	Peru (A)	PE 1
Denmark (A)	1 DAN	Portugal (A)	1 POR
Dominica (HC)	DOM 1A	Quebec (Canada) (AG)	QUE 1
Ecuador (A)	1 ECU	Russia (A)	1 RF
El Salvador (A)	ELS 1	Seychelles (HC)	SEY 1
Finland (A)	SF 10	Slovakia (A)	SVK 1A
Gambia (HC)	1 GAM	Slovenia (A)	SLO 1A
Georgia (A)	1 GRG	Sri Lanka (HC)	1 SL
Iceland (A)	IC 1	Sudan (A)	SUD 1
Kazakhstan (A)	1 KSN	Tonga (HC)	1 TON
Kenya (HC)	1 KEN	Ukraine (A)	UKR 1
Korea (Republic of) (A)	1 ROK	Western Australia (AG)	WA 1
Kuwait (A)	1 KUW		

In the Republic of Ireland, diplomatic cars have normal Dublin registration marks but these are often displayed with the extra letters CD on the numberplate.

Oval Plates

A white oval plate or sticker with black lettering displayed on (usually the back of) a vehicle travelling abroad identifies the vehicle's country of origin. Oval plates, however, are not always used and many countries now display their international identification letters on a panel as part of the numberplate, often accompanied by the national flag.

A	Austria	CI	Côte d'Ivoire	G	Gabon
AFG	Afghanistan	CL	Sri Lanka	GB	United Kingdom
AL	Albania	CO	Colombia	GBA	Alderney
AM	Armenia	CR	Costa Rica	GBG	Guernsey
AND	Andorra	CY	Cyprus	GBJ	Jersey
AUS	Australia	CZ	Czech Republic	GBM	Isle of Man
AZ	Azerbaijan			GBZ	Gibraltar
		D	Germany	GCA	Guatemala
B	Belgium	DK	Denmark	GE	Georgia
BD	Bangladesh	DOM	Dominican	GH	Ghana
BDS	Barbados		Republic	GR	Greece
BF	Burkina Faso	DY	Benin	GUY	Guyana
BG	Bulgaria	DZ	Algeria		
BIH	Bosnia-			H	Hungary
	Herzogovina	E	Spain	HK	Hong Kong
BOL	Bolivia	EAK	Kenya	HKJ	Jordan
BR	Brazil	EAT	Tanzania	HR	Croatia
BRN	Bahrain		(Tanganyika)		
BRU	Brunei	EAU	Uganda	I	Italy
BS	Bahamas	EAZ	Tanzania	IL	Israel
BUR	Myanmar		(Zanzibar)	IND	India
BVI	British Virgin	EC	Ecuador	IR	Iran
	Islands	ES	El Salvador	IRL	Ireland
BY	Belarus	EST	Estonia	IRQ	Iraq
BZ	Belize	ET	Egypt	IS	Iceland
		ETH	Ethiopia		
C	Cuba			J	Japan
CAM	Cameroon	F	France	JA	Jamaica
CD	Corps	FIN	Finland		
	Diplomatique	FJI	Fiji	K	Cambodia
	(see page 100)	FL	Liechtenstein	KS	Kyrgyzstan
CDN	Canada	FO	Faroe Islands	KWT	Kuwait
CH	Switzerland	FSM	Micronesia	KZ	Kazakhstan

L	Luxembourg	Q	Qatar	T	Thailand
LAO	Laos			TCH	Chad
LAR	Libya	RA	Argentina	TG	Togo
LB	Liberia	RB	Botswana	TJ	Tajikistan
LS	Lesotho	RC	Taiwan	TMN	Turkmenistan
LT	Lithuania	RCA	Central African	TN	Tunisia
LV	Latvia		Republic	TR	Turkey
		RCB	Congo	TT	Trinidad and
M	Malta	RCH	Chile		Tobago
MA	Morocco	RG	Guinea		
MAL	Malaysia	RH	Haiti	UA	Ukraine
MC	Monaco	RI	Indonesia	USA	United States of
MD	Moldova	RIM	Mauritania		America
MEX	Mexico	RL	Lebanaon	UZ	Uzbekistan
MGL	Mongolia	RM	Madagascar		
MK	Macedonia	RMM	Mali	V	Vatican
MOC	Mozambique	RN	Niger	VN	Vietnam
MS	Mauritius	RO	Romania		
MW	Malawi	ROK	South Korea	WAG	Gambia
		ROU	Uruguay	WAL	Sierra Leone
N	Norway	RP	Philippines	WD	Dominica
NA	Netherlands	RSM	San Marino	WG	Grenada
	Antilles	RU	Burundi	WL	St Lucia
NAM	Namibia	RUS	Russia	WS	Samoa
NAU	Nauru	RWA	Rwanda	WV	St Vincent and the
NEP	Nepal				Grenadines
NGR	Nigeria				
NIC	Nicaragua	S	Sweden		
NL	Netherlands	SA	Saudi Arabia	YMN	Yemen
NZ	New Zealand	SD	Swaziland	YU	Yugoslavia
		SGP	Singapore	YV	Venezuela
P	Portugal	SK	Slovakia		
PA	Panama	SME	Suriname		
PE	Peru	SN	Senegal	Z	Zambia
PK	Pakistan	SLO	Slovenia	ZA	South Africa
PL	Poland	SO	Somalia	ZRE	Democratic
PNG	Papua New	SUD	Sudan		Republic of
	Guinea	SY	Seychelles		Congo
PY	Paraguay	SYR	Syria	ZW	Zimbabwe

Tax Discs

Vehicle taxation in the United Kingdom was introduced in 1909-10 and was based on the horsepower (or, very roughly, the engine size) of the vehicle, charges starting at £2.10s (£2.50) a year for vehicles under $6^{1}/2$ hp. The revenue from this tax was to be used for road improvement, hence its name 'Road Fund Licence'. In 1921 the tax was set at £1 a year per unit of horsepower and could be paid either annually (January to December) or quarterly (January to March, April to June, etc.). At the same time, tax discs were introduced as proof of payment and were required to be displayed on the windscreen or nearside of the vehicle. The first discs (1921-2) had black printing on a plain white background but various colours were used from 1923 onwards.

The 'horsepower' rating was replaced in 1948 by a flat rate annual charge of £10. This rate has now increased to £160 with reductions for cars with an engine size of 1549 cc or less, or low carbon dioxide emission. In 1961 the taxation periods were altered so that a vehicle could be taxed for 12 or 4 months, beginning in any month. This rule was amended in 1981 to 12 or 6 months. Different rates applied to heavy goods and other specialist types of vehicle.

Current tax discs (licences) for new vehicles in the UK can be of two basic types, 'local office generated' or 'dealer generated'. Those issued by DVLA Local Offices (Great Britain) include a twelve-digit number of which the first digit is the last figure of the year, the next three digits are the day of the year, the next three are the office code number (see page 92), the next two are the machine number and the final three are the receipt line number. Thus, a tax disc displaying 2177 392 06018 would be the 18th disc issued by machine number 6 at Cardiff Local Office on 26 June 2002 (the 177th day of 2002). Discs issued by the eight DVLNI offices are almost identical to those in Great Britain except that they include the words NORTHERN IRELAND printed in white round the lower rim, the 'hand' emblem of Ulster in the lower centre and, on the bottom line, the first three letters of the issuing office followed by the serial number of the disc, e.g. BEL 63695818 issued in Belfast (letters 'lic' signify DVLNI postal licences, e.g. lic 81263538).

Licences issued by dealers under the Automated First Registration and Licensing (AFRL) scheme (throughout Great Britain and soon to be introduced in Northern Ireland) can be recognised by a circular DEALER stamp with the dealer's individual number, e.g. 4528 for Gordons of Bolton. Normal renewal tax discs are issued and stamped by local post offices.

Tax discs in the Republic of Ireland are similar in basic design to those in the UK but must be displayed alongside an insurance disc (or rectangle). The Isle of Man and Guernsey (including Alderney) use their own distinctively designed discs whereas Jersey does not issue them at all, having abandoned motor taxation in 1994.

Great Britain

Northern Ireland

Diplomatic (UK)

Republic of Ireland

Guernsey

Isle of Man

Books / Newsletters

BOOKS FOR THE ENTHUSIAST

CAR NUMBERS by Noël Woodall and Brian Heaton. The ultimate directory of interesting registration marks, this is an illustrated hard-backed book with more than 1,000 pages (16 in colour). It lists 102,000 numbers, many with owners' names and localities, and includes DVLA 'Classic' issues with their auction prices. Latest edition 2000. ISBN 0950253790. Contact: Noël Woodall, The Blenheim Suite, Ribby Hall, Wrea Green, PRESTON PR4 2PA.

REGISTRATION PLATES OF THE WORLD by Neil Parker, John Weeks and the late Reg Wilson. An 800-page compendium of detailed information covering every country in the world including current and earlier series with relevant historical notes. Most types of plate illustrated and identified. A must for the international enthusiast. Latest edition 1994, ISBN 0950273554 (hardback); next edition early 2003, ISBN 0950273570 (hardback). Contact: Europlate, Plas Rheged, Creech St Michael, TAUNTON TA3 5NX.

THE INTERPOL GUIDE TO VEHICLE REGISTRATION PLATES by Neil Parker and John Weeks. Contains descriptions of registration plates of all European countries (and neighbouring countries in Africa and Asia) with illustrations in full colour. Loose-leaf format in a hard binder. Last updated November 2002. Published by Keesing Reference Systems BV, Amsterdam. ISBN 9080583715. Contact: Europlate, Plas Rheged, Creech St Michael, TAUNTON TA3 5NX.

LOCATIONS OF SURVIVING LOCAL TAXATION OFFICE RECORDS. A 24-page booklet listing pre-1974 licensing authorities (Local Taxation Offices) in the U.K. and Republic of Ireland with full details, including addresses and telephone numbers, of the present whereabouts of any surviving registration records. Reissued April 2002, £3 post free. Contact: The Kithead Trust, De Salis Drive, Hampton Lovett, DROITWICH WR9 0QE.

GLASS'S GUIDE INDEX OF REGISTRATION MARKS. This book is used principally by car dealers. It lists registration mark series issued during the past eleven years in the UK and Isle of Man, showing year letter, three-letter mark, place of origin and precise dates of beginning and end of each series. Latest edition 2002. Contact: Glass's Information Services Ltd., 1 Princes Road, WEYBRIDGE KT13 9TU.

FANATICAL ABOUT NUMBER PLATES by Ruby Speechley. Through personal stories from the customers of leading number plate dealer Regtransfers, this 300-page hardback book reveals the reasons why plates have become more than just a number to so many people. Fully illustrated in colour, the book also includes a brief history of registrations, details of the new-format numbers and information about investing in number plates and protecting the rights to a number. Published 2002, price £28.00. ISBN 0954309103. Contact: Regtransfers, 139 High Street South, DUNSTABLE LU6 3SS. Website: www.regtransfers.co.uk

HOW TO TRACE THE HISTORY OF YOUR CAR by Philip Riden. Written for the owner or enthusiast wishing to know more about a vehicle's origins, this book contains a history of vehicle licensing in the British Isles, together with an index of registrations, who first issued them and where original documents are now kept. Latest edition 1998, price £5.95. ISBN 1898937257. Contact: Merton Priory Press Ltd., 67 Merthyr Road, Whitchurch, CARDIFF CF14 1DD.

GREAT BRITAIN ROAD TAX DISCS 1921-2000 by R.H. Champion, E.J. Hitchings and M. Brice. This 20-page A4 size monograph includes a history of motor taxation from the earliest times, descriptions of annual and quarterly tax disc designs and details of special issues and trade licences. It also features four pages of excellent colour illustrations and a table showing colours and patterns of discs year by year. Published 2000, price £4.50. Contact: Tony Hall, The Revenue Society of Great Britain, 57 Brandles Road, LETCHWORTH SG6 2JA. Email: rsgb.hall@talk21.com

NEWSLETTERS

1903 AND ALL THAT is a quarterly newsletter which deals with all aspects of vehicle registrations. For a sample copy and subscription details please send a large SAE (33p stamp) to John Harrison, 175 Hillyfields, LOUGHTON IG10 2PW.

REGISTRATION NEWSLETTER is published every six months and contains detailed information for the dedicated British registration enthusiast, including latest number news and observations countrywide. It also gives complete listings of items included in DVLA number auctions. Contact: Graham Cox, 93 Benwell Road, LONDON N7 7BW.

For other newsletters see 'Societies' section on page 109.

Acknowledgments / Picture Credits

The author wishes to acknowledge his indebtedness to the late Les Newall for his help with the 'Authorities' section of this book and for permission to quote details of Irish registrations from his book 'A History of Vehicle Registration in the United Kingdom' (now sadly out of print); to Noël Woodall and Brian Heaton for information from their book 'Where's it from? When was it issued?' (also out of print); to John Harrison for proof-reading and valuable advice; to the heads of many diplomatic missions in London for information about their cars; to many city, town, county and other councils for their help; and to Earl Russell, Graham Cox, Paul Haynes, Dr Heike Hoppe, Peter Jarman, Colin Leadill, Trevor Mitchell, Neil Parker, Ian Robertson, Michael Robinson, Robin Taylor, Ivan Thornley, John Weeks, Noël Woodall, the Association of Old Vehicle Clubs in Northern Ireland Ltd (AOVC), the Canadian High Commission (London), the Defence Logistics Organisation, Europlate (European Registration Plate Association), the Honorary Consulate of Benin (London), the Museum of Army Transport (Beverley), Nippy Taxis (Scarborough), the Paraguayan Embassy (London), Peter Kelly's (Scarborough), Prontaprint Scarborough, the Road Transport Fleet Data Society, the Royal Air Force Museum (Hendon), Roy Tatler Motors (Scilly) and Stones Fuel Oils Ltd (Malton).

Picture Credits (t=top, m=middle, b=bottom, l=left, r=right). Page 2t National Motor Museum (Beaulieu), 5 Graeme Dixon, 7 Dorset Natural History and Archaeological Society, 13tr National Museums and Galleries of Northern Ireland (Ulster Folk and Transport Museum), 13bl Drive TV, 14tr/br Gerry Costello Photography (Galway), 16t/m John and Mary Nicholls, 20m Regtransfers, 40 John Crawley Collection, 45t PA Photos, 45ml Sydney Eden, 45mr Steve Wakeham, 45b Hotshots Photography (London), 46t Midlothian Council, 46m Leicester City Council, 46b Shrewsbury & Atcham Borough Council, 47t London Borough of Bromley, 47ml Burnley Borough Council, 47mr Chesterfield Borough Council, 47b Exeter City Council, 48tl Drive TV, 48tr/bl/49tr/ml Gerry Costello Photography (Galway), 48br PR Section - Defence Forces Ireland, 49mr Drive TV, 49b Ivan Thornley, 50ml Falles Hire Cars (Jersey), 50mr Jacksons, Mercedes-Benz dealers of Jersey, 50b States of Alderney Marketing, 53br Ivan Thornley, 54tr Rolls Royce & Bentley Motor Cars Ltd, 55t J.C.Bamford Excavators Ltd, 55b Drive TV, 81t/b,82t/b Courtesy of the Director, National Army Museum, London, 81ml Steve Crampton, 81mr Peter Jarman, 84t Veteran Car Sales, 86t/mr(lower)/87ml(upper) Ivan Thornley, 86mr(upper) Desmond Shortt, 86b Dovercourt Tax Free (London), 87tr/105mr Tommy Robinson Ltd (Castlebar), 87ml(lower)/b/105bl Doyle Motors Ltd (Guernsey), 87mr Hudson Motor Company (Jersey), 105tr Trevor Mitchell, 105ml The Canadian High Commission, 105br Michael Car Centre (IOM), Back Cover (913 AZM) Gerry Costello Photography (Galway). All other photographs were taken by the author with Pentax cameras.

MOD vehicles at RAF Linton-on-Ouse (42tl,tr, 82mr, 83tl,tr,br) photographed by kind permission of Group Captain K L Cornfield OBE MA RAF, Station Commander with assistance afforded by Graham Giles, Motor Transport Officer, Vosper Thorneycroft Aerospace Ltd.

SOCIETIES

REGISTRATION NUMBERS CLUB. Founded in January 1977 by a group of enthusiasts in the North of England. Its original aim was to ensure the continuation of cherished registration transfers at a time when these were being threatened. The club welcomes all cherished number enthusiasts and owners. It publishes a quarterly illustrated magazine and organises an annual rally. Contact: Steve Waldenberg, PO Box MT12, LEEDS LS17 7UD

ROAD TRANSPORT FLEET DATA SOCIETY. Formed in 1980, this society investigates the vehicles and activities of British transport fleets, including military vehicles and those operated by councils, emergency services, hire firms and other large companies. Members are provided with two regular newsletters 'Council Vehicle News' and 'Public Utilities Bulletin' and the society also publishes booklets of British military serials and fleet lists of council vehicles. Contact: Fleet Data, 18 Poplar Close, BIGGLESWADE SG18 0EW.

EUROPLATE (the European Registration Plate Association) was formed in 1972 and now has around 350 members in 30 countries. It welcomes all those interested in registration marks and plates worldwide. A quarterly newsletter is circulated to members and a convention is held every two years. The association also publishes 'Registration Plates of the World' (see page 106). Contact: Europlate, Plas Rheged, Creech St Michael, TAUNTON TA3 5NX.

ADDRESSES

Driver & Vehicle Licensing Agency (DVLA), Longview Road, SWANSEA
SA6 7JL. Telephone 01792 782341. Website: www.dvla.gov.uk

DVLA Vehicle Enquiries. Telephone 0870 240 0010.
Email: vehicles.dvla@gtnet.gov.uk

DVLA Sale of Marks (for cherished numbers). Telephone 0870 6000 142
Website: www.dvla-som.co.uk

Driver & Vehicle Licensing Northern Ireland (DVLNI), County Hall,
Castlerock Road, COLERAINE BT51 3TA. Telephone 028 7034 1461.
Website: www.dvlni.gov.uk   Email: dvlni@doeni.gov.uk

DVLA Local Offices, DVLNI offices and offshore islands offices: see page 93.
Republic of Ireland offices: see pages 96 and 97

Glossary

AFRL - Automated First Registration and Licensing. A system introduced in 1994 whereby new registration marks can be issued by dealers without involvement of DVLA Local Offices.

Age Indentifier - The numerals in the middle of a new-style (September 2001) mark in Great Britain denoting the six-month period of issue. See also Prefix and Suffix.

Age-related Mark - A newly-issued mark which appears to be an appropriate age for the vehicle for which it is issued, either as a replacement in a cherished transfer or for a used vehicle being newly registered, e.g. because it is imported, ex-military or ex-agricultural.

Autonumerology - The study of vehicle registration marks.

CD - Corps Diplomatique (Diplomatic Corps). Letters shown on an oval plate sometimes displayed on diplomats' cars.

Cherished Mark - A mark, often transferred from vehicle to vehicle, which has a special significance.

Cherished Transfer - Transfer of a cherished mark from one vehicle to another.

Classic Car - A collectable or historically interesting car manufactured from January 1931 onwards.

Classic Collection - Marks, not previously issued, auctioned by DVLA.

CNDA - Cherished Numbers Dealers Association. An organisation founded by dealers in cherished marks for the promotion of high trading standards.

Custom Mark - Mark, not previously issued, auctioned by DVLA. Similar to those in Classic Collection but less expensive because less attractive.

Donor Vehicle - The vehicle from which a cherished mark is transferred.

DVLA - Driver and Vehicle Licensing Agency. The central computerised agency in Swansea for drivers' and vehicle licences in Great Britain. Known, until April 1990, as the DVLC (Driver and Vehicle Licensing Centre) which is still the name of the building it occupies.

DVLNI - Driver and Vehicle Licensing Northern Ireland. The computerised centre in Coleraine for drivers' and vehicle licences in Northern Ireland.

Edwardian Car - A car manufactured between January 1905 and December 1918.

ERM - Equipment Registration Mark. The official name for a UK military registration mark.

GIM - General Identification Mark. The old name for a trade plate.

Great Britain - England, Wales and Scotland.

Local Memory Tag - The first letter of a new-style (September 2001) mark in Great Britain denoting one of nineteen licensing areas.

Log Book - The unofficial name for a Vehicle Registration Document (V5) or an old-style (pre-1974) Registration Book (RF60 or VE60).

LTO - Local Taxation Office. The office of a county, county borough or larger Scottish burgh council responsible for the issue of registration marks until centralisation in 1974.

LVLO - Local Vehicle Licensing Office. One of eight local licensing offices in Northern Ireland. Also an old name for a DVLA Local Office in Great Britain.

MIRAD - Member of the Institute of Registration Agents and Dealers.

MOT Test - Popular name for the annual test administered by the Vehicle Inspectorate, a division of the Department of Transport, Local Government and the Regions (DTLR). MOT stands for the former Ministry of Transport.

Numberplate - The plastic or metal plate on which a registration mark is displayed.

Oval Plate - An oval-shaped international identification plate or sticker, usually displayed on the back of a vehicle or on its numberplate(s), showing the country of registration of the vehicle.

Prefix - (a) The first letter of a three-letter mark.
(b) A letter at the beginning of a mark issued between 1983 and 2001 to show the year of registration (or half-year from 1998 onwards).

Recipient Vehicle (or Receiving Vehicle)- The vehicle to which a cherished mark is transferred.

Replacement Mark - A mark issued for a donor vehicle in place of a mark which has been transferred from the vehicle.

Re-registration - A registration mark issued for a vehicle in place of its original mark. Another name for a replacement mark.

Retention Certificate - A document (V778) certifying the right to retain a registration mark not currently displayed on a vehicle.

Select Registration - A mark with age-identifier or year-prefix sold by telephone or through the internet by DVLA.

Suffix - A letter at the end of a mark issued between 1963 and 1983 to show the year of registration.

Trade Plate - A numberplate displaying a mark for temporary use on an unlicensed vehicle.

UK - United Kingdom (England, Wales, Scotland and Northern Ireland)

V5 - A modern Vehicle Registration Document, often called a log book.

Veteran Vehicle - (a) Strictly, a car manufactured no later than December 1904, but cars from 1905 to 1918 (Edwardian) are often generally called veterans and their owners are eligible for membership of the Veteran Car Club (VCC). (b) A motorcycle manufactured no later than December 1914.

Vintage Vehicle - A car manufactured between January 1919 and December 1930 or a motorcycle manufactured between January 1915 and December 1930.

VRO - Vehicle Registration Office (in the Republic of Ireland). Also an old name for a DVLA Local Office in Great Britain.

Index